M000028219

Caring for
Creation in Your
Own Backyard

Caring for Creation in Your Own Backyard

Loren and Mary Ruth Wilkinson

Regent College Publishing
Vancouver, British Columbia

CARING FOR CREATION IN YOUR OWN BACKYARD
Copyright © 1992 by Loren and Mary Ruth Wilkinson

Passages from Scripture used in this work are from the New International Version, copyright © 1973, 1978, 1984 by the New York International Bible Society. Used by permission of Zondervan Bible Publishers.

First published by Vine Books, an imprint of Servant Publications
P.O. Box 8617
Ann Arbor, Michigan 48107 (ISBN 0-89283-715-9)

Reproduced 1997 with permission by Regent College Publishing, an imprint of the Regent College Bookstore,
5800 University Boulevard, Vancouver, B.C. V6T 2E4

Printed in Canada

All rights reserved. No part of this publication may be reproduced, stored in a retrieval system, or transmitted, in any form or by any means, electronic, mechanical, photocopying, recording of otherwise, without the prior written permission of the publisher, except in the case of brief quotations embodied in critical articles and reviews.

Library of Congress Cataloging-in-Publication Data

Wilkinson, Loren
  Caring for creation in your own backyard / Loren and Mary Ruth Wilkinson

    reprint. Caring for creation in your own backyard: over 100 things Christian families can do to help the earth / Loren and Mary Ruth Wilkinson

  268 p. 22 cm.
  Includes bibliographical references (p. 263-264) and index.
  1. Environmental protection -- Citizen participation. 2. Stewardship, Christian. I. Wilkinson, Mary Ruth, 1942- II. Title.
TD171.7 W55 1995

ISBN 1-57383-057-7

Contents

PREFACE

IN PRINT TODAY ARE DOZENS OF BOOKS which give good advice on caring for creation. The titles are variations on a theme: "Fifty [or 100, or 365, or 1001] Things You Can Do to Save the Planet." When Servant Publications asked us if we would write a book that would add a Christian version to that burgeoning list, at first we weren't very excited about the idea. The earth is the Lord's, whether or not we acknowledge him, and good stewardship is the same whether done by a Christian or an atheist. Environmentally-wise habits are good in themselves, and it seemed to us that if Christians don't already practice them, they could (and ought to) learn such habits from "secular" sources.

But when we thought a bit more about it and looked at some of those many books of down-to-earth environmental advice, we changed our minds. For, excellent as they are, they have a common flaw: the advice they offer sidesteps some crucial questions.

Why *should* we care for the earth? If we're just part of a long cosmic accident, what can words like ought and should possibly mean? And stewardship—which implies responsible use—also implies responsibility *to* a master. But the confused modern understandings of "nature" or "environment" or "the cosmic dance" leave out the Creator and thus leave concepts of stewardship rootless.

Another thing missing from most contemporary books of environmental advice is *joy*. The element of urgent concern has almost overshadowed delight at the inexhaustible gift of creation. If we become so concerned with saving the earth that we fail to take pleasure in its textures, scents, shapes, and tastes, we are failing in our stewardship almost as much as if we destroyed those things. So we hope in this book also to encourage worship of the Creator and pleasure in his work.

If the mountains leap and the trees of the field clap their hands, why should we creatures made in his image stay silent?

There are many dangers in reading—and writing—a book like this. One of the greatest is that both writers and readers take its many suggestions—sometimes tentative and trivial—far too seriously; so that we experience guilt every time we do anything that has an impact on creation. But another danger is that we conclude that the earth and its problems are so vast that nothing we do can make any difference. So here's some general advice on how to think about and act on this book's suggestions.

1. Don't try to do everything at once.
2. Avoid over-simplifying complex issues: don't become an "environmental fundamentalist."
3. Doing will win others over more than talking.
4. Laugh at yourself.
5. Prioritize: people and their feelings always come before projects, favorite problems.
6. Don't despair at the magnitude of the problems; the earth is the Lord's.
7. Don't make an environmental ideology the center of your faith.
8. Don't leave the Christian mind behind in approaching environmental problems.
9. Wherever you are, and at whatever stage of life, you can always do *something*.
10. Don't become so occupied with problems that you fail to see the glory of creation and the Creator.

We're grateful to lots of people for help with this book: Erik, our son, who often came home from a hard day of carpentry to find his parents so busy writing about the values of "cooking from scratch" that they didn't have time to cook supper. He cooked superb meals during the writing and never complained.

Heidi and Paul, our daughter and son-in-law, who provided us with a thorough critique of our first draft of the book and lots of helpful suggestions along the way.

Madeleine Sabourin and Libby Brooks, our teaching assistants at Regent College, who chased after books in Vancouver libraries and looked after us in many other ways.

Shannon Lythgoe, a kindred spirit on Galiano Island, who typed, cooked, concocted, and generally encouraged.

Our parents, Ruth and Kenneth Kantzer and Elda and Edman Wilkinson, who have lived lightly and joyously in creation and passed some of that joy on to their children.

We appreciate the help of other aspects of creation: Broonie, the puppy of indeterminate origin who joined us at the beginning of this project and who spent many boring days neglected while we wrote about caring for creatures; our gardens, and fruit trees, which produced bountifully with little work from us, reminding us daily of the Creator's goodness; and the daily progression of tides, clouds, herons, eagles, kingfishers, and occasional stray sheep outside our bedroom window, reminding us repeatedly of the goodness and grandeur of God's earth.

Borrowing Paul's words in Acts 14:17, we give thanks to God our Creator and redeemer, who through a busy spring and summer showed kindness by giving us rain from heaven, and crops in their seasons; he provided us with plenty of food, and filled our hearts with joy.

We hope he fills your heart with joy as you read this book and continue in your task and privilege of caring for creation, as the Creator has cared for all of us.

The Way of the Cross
and the Circle of the Earth

At the still point of the turning world....
Except for the point, the still point,
There would be no dance, and there is only the dance.
　　　　　　　　　—T.S. Eliot, "Burnt Norton"

Human beings have broken out of the circle of life.... The end
result is the environmental crisis, a crisis of survival. Once more,
to survive, we must close the circle. We must learn how to restore
to nature the wealth that we borrow from it.
　　　　　　　　　—Barry Commoner, *The Closing Circle*

THE MOST POWERFUL SYMBOL in our time is the picture of the
earth from space. Thirty years ago we had no such view. But
that image of the planet seems to hold for many today their
only hope of wholeness. Individual life, they say, is meaningless; what counts is the health of the planet, and finding our
meaning in its health.

Christians too are moved by these pictures of our planet,
but are not convinced that our only hope is in the planet's
health. "What does it profit," we say, "if we save the whole
earth and lose our own souls?" Our hope is centered on
another symbol, the cross. The cross expresses God's good
news to men and women.

Is the cross good news for the rest of creation as well? Can
the two symbols—of the earth (a circle) and the cross—be re-
conciled? Can there be such a thing as a "Christian environmentalist"? We are convinced the answer to these questions

is yes, and in this book we describe some ways we can put that conviction into action. But first we need to think a little more about what is implied by these two symbols, circle and cross, and the relationships and tensions between them.

First the circle. The earth is round, and it is full of cycles. Living things die and rot into soil, which nourishes more living things. Rain falls on mountains, where it drains into rivers, which flow into the sea, which evaporates into clouds, which carry rain again to the mountains. The carbon dioxide we exhale is taken in by plants, which expire oxygen, which we inhale and then exhale as carbon dioxide. For all these cycles the circle is a good symbol.

Christian thinking is centered on the cross. Geometrically, the cross is the intersection of two straight lines, a horizontal and a vertical. Instead of one line, turning again and again in a circle, the Christian sees that the earth is not eternal. For another line intersects ours from outside. The cross refers to the place where God's perspective has intersected ours most clearly. The execution of one man at a particular place and time is the midpoint, the crux: the intersection of eternal and temporal, God's time and ours.

Many environmentalists are understandably suspicious of this Christian view of time and of the Christian conviction that there is another reality intersecting ours. They say that it has made Christians other-worldly, neglectful of the needs of the earth, too likely to use the earth only as a backdrop for the human drama of eternal salvation. Thus many are attracted by religions that try to find human purpose through reentry into the cycle, stressing reincarnation, return to nature, or restoration of harmony with the cycles of the ecosphere.

The biblical view recognizes the reality of the cycles of nature. They are described very well in the book of Ecclesiastes:

Generations come and generations go,
    but the earth remains forever.
The sun rises and the sun sets,

and hurries back to where it rises.
The wind blows to the south
    and turns to the north;
round and round it goes,
    ever returning on its course.
All streams flow into the sea,
    yet the sea is never full.
To the place the streams come from,
    there they return again.   —Ecclesiastes 1:4-7

And though within those cycles of the earth there is room for every kind of activity ("a time to be born and a time to die, a time to plant and a time to uproot, a time to kill and a time to heal..." [Eccl 3:2-3]) and for great happiness and good, God has "set eternity in the hearts of men [and women]" (Eccl 3:11). We are not satisfied with the cycles. For all the beauty of the earth and its circling life, it does not bring its own meaning with it. Thus the refrain of Ecclesiastes—"Meaningless [vanity]! Meaningless!... Everything is meaningless!" (Eccl 12:8).

Creation itself is neither meaningless nor empty, but it lacks a center: the center provided by recognizing that creation is not just "nature" or "resources" or "the environment." The writer of Ecclesiastes both concludes and answers his lament with words particularly well-suited for our time: "Remember your Creator."

For it is only when we think of the earth as "creation" that we can think rightly about caring for it. The circle, in its completeness, is a good symbol for creation. But it is also a zero, a cipher, an emptiness. So perhaps we can learn from an ancient Christian symbol, the circle centered on the cross. Sometimes it is known as the "Celtic Cross" or the "St. Andrew's Cross." It expresses a profound truth: the God whom we meet in Christ at the cross is also the God of creation. And just as the arms of the cross enclose and intersect the circle, so also Redemption includes creation.

Names for the Earth

What *is* this thing we are concerned to care for? How do we speak of it? Several names have been popular at different times. Three of them provide us with a kind of historical summary of changing human attitudes.

NATURE

The first (and oldest) of such words is nature. It is related to words referring to birth (like *natal* and *nativity*), and reflects the mysterious fertility of the earth, which seems to bring forth life of its own accord. ("Nature" religions worship the earth and worship fertility.) Thus nature, "that which gives birth," has often been spoken of as a mother: a kind but impersonal goddess to which we can attribute everything that comes into being. Recently *nature* has been used as a synonym for *evolution*, when people want to attribute purpose to what (strictly speaking) can only be a random process. Even more recently the old idea of nature as a goddess Nature has been given an old name, Gaia, the Greek name for the goddess of the earth.

RESOURCES

There is a more modern way of thinking of the earth: as "resources," something to be used. Thus we speak of departments of "natural resources" and of "conserving resources." The trouble, though, with thinking of the earth as resources is that it implies that its main purpose is for human use. This way of thinking (and speaking) of the earth came into prominence when the "new world" was discovered and seemed to open up great sources of riches. It was augmented by the scientific and industrial revolutions, which gave us new knowledge about how the world was made and how it could give us power. Coal, iron ore, falling water, uranium, plants, and animals are seen no longer as just part of creation, but as *resources* for our use.

ENVIRONMENT

Largely as a reaction against the damage done by regarding the earth as resources, we have recently come to speak of it as "the environment." The word reflects our growing sense of interconnectedness: we do not live in isolation, but in an "environment" made up of living and nonliving things. Soil, air, water, energy, plants, and animals are all linked in cycles of exchange.

The problem with *environment* is that it says either too little or too much. It says too little when we mean by it *our* (human) environment. Then we are back to regarding all things simply as resources for us. But it means too much when it means "everything connected to everything else" in an equal and undifferentiated web. Then we have no place to stand: we are just part of an endless cosmic process without beginning, end, purpose, or center. In this "environmentalist" view we are just one more part of the web, acting and acted upon. But one part of a web can hardly be "steward" of another.

The renewed relationship with the Creator which we have through the cross does not leave creation behind: We are saved *for* creation, not *out of it.* Yet our relationship with the Creator means that we are not simply part of the cycles of creation. We also have a relationship of responsibility with the Creator. And that relationship implies stewardship: *of* creation and *for* both creation and Creator.

"Stewardship" (from an Old English word meaning "sty-warden" or pig-keeper) translates the Greek word *oikonomia*, which means "keeper of the household." The word is also translated "economics": economics *is* stewardship, and vice versa. In Greek the word contains *oikos*, which means household, and shows up in a more recent word, *ecology*, coined in the nineteenth century to describe the science of the relationship of living things to their environment: the whole *ecumene*, or earthly dwelling place. So "economics" not only means stewardship, but it is closely related to ecology: both deal with the whole *oikos* or household of creation. We have tried to suggest some of the richness of this word in the word *earthkeeping*, which suggests not only the everydayness of "housekeeping" but the breadth of our larger home, the whole created earth.

The word *stewardship* is used with increasing frequency today to describe the care of the earth. It is a good word, and it describes a crucial human task. But we think that it can have meaning only if we approach the cycles of creation from the standpoint that it *is* creation, and that we draw strength for the task from the ultimate servant of creation, who is Christ.

In this book we give lots of specific advice about caring for the earth. We are concerned about the whole planet. But it's discouraging business, caring for a whole planet. So although we need to know about the planet, our care for it begins at home, in "our own backyard." That can be the literal backyard where we raise our garden or the extended backyard where our food and fuel come from and our garbage goes.

It is a cosmic task. But we approach it a day at a time: with love (for creation is rich and varied, a waterfall of gifts to us from the Creator) and with humility (for it is God who made us, and not we ourselves, and most of our attempts to mend or improve on God's creation only mar it).

The words Jeremiah conveyed to exiles in Babylon are good for us to hear when we face such a task: "This is what the Lord Almighty, the God of Israel, says to all those I carried into exile from Jerusalem to Babylon: 'Build houses and settle down; plant gardens and eat what they produce... seek the peace and prosperity of the city to which I have carried you into exile'" (Jer 29:4-5,7).

The Jewish people were called to a double awareness: first, to make the place where they lived *home.* We too are called to the daily, weekly, yearly task of tending families, gardens, communities, and the created world with our whole heart. Thus we recall these tasks in a cyclical, season-by-season way. But they (and we) are reminded that, lovely as the earth is, it is not the only reality. The cycles of creation and daily life are intersected and centered by the cross. The cross is the symbol of our greatest failing: our rebellion against the Creator. But it also points to our ultimate fulfillment: a restored relationship to the Creator, through his own suffering.

Thus as we think seasonally about the tasks of caring for creation, we can think also about the new life we have in Christ: the one story of salvation unfolding through history and ultimately restoring us to Creator and creation alike.

The real work of planet-saving will be small, humble, and humbling, and (insofar as it involves love) pleasing and rewarding. Its jobs will be too many to count, too many to report, too many to be publicly noticed or rewarded, too small to make anyone rich or famous.

—Wendell Berry, "Out of Your Car, Off Your Horse," *The Atlantic Monthly* (February 1991) 63.

PART ONE

AUTUMN

THINGS TO DO

- Begin to speak of the earth as "creation" rather than "nature," "resources," or "the environment."
- Stop your home from leaking heat.
- Learn how to be comfortable at a lower temperature.
- Plant deciduous trees around your home for shade in summer and sun in winter.
- Focus warmth—and the family—around the fireplace on winter evenings.
- Buy energy-efficient appliances.
- Shift from clothes-dryer to clothes-line and clothes-rack.
- Turn down the setting on your hot-water heater.
- Insulate your hot water tank and the water lines leading from it.
- Install "low-flow" shower heads with turn-off valves.
- Consider alternate hot water systems such as demand heaters and solar heaters.
- Turn off the lights when they're not being used.
- Switch to flourescent and compact flourescent lights.
- Learn to live with a range of light and shadow.
- Get in the habit of using public transportation.
- Save gas by the way you drive.
- Turn the water off while soaping, shaving, and brushing your teeth.
- Check for and fix leaky toilets.
- Install "toilet dams" (or plastic water-filled bottles) to save flush water.
- Water lawns efficiently.
- Refuse unnecessary packaging when shopping.
- Buy in bulk to save packaging.
- Choose refillable and recyclable containers for food purchases.
- Stow away your own supply of shopping bags and containers in the car for shopping trips.
- Battle with bargains you don't really need.

- Wage war on whimsy purchases when shopping.
- Banish browse buying—or shopping as entertainment.
- Hold out against the hidden persuaders of advertising.
- Refuse to buy throwaways.
- Purchase hand-operated and/or multi-purpose gadgetry for the kitchen (avoid one-use electric gadgets).
- Say "No" to and find substitutes for household poisons such as dangerous pesticides, aerosols, toxic cleaners.
- Use rechargeable batteries.
- Reuse paper garbage to meet your own paper needs, such as scratchpads, envelopes, wrapping paper...
- Use glass jars for storing bulk foods, refrigerated leftovers, and workshop collections of nuts, bolts, etc.
- Invent round-the-house reuses for plastic containers (as frozen food containers, plant pots, etc.).
- Give away your wealth of paper and plastic shopping bags to thrift stores.
- Save bacon (and other meat) drippings to make soap.
- Save juices from cooking vegetables to make soup.
- Discover new ways to make good use of things you normally throw away.
- Reuse others' good throwaways: use garage sales, thrift stores, and your own back alley.
- Set up a household garbage separation system.
- Recycle all glass, metal, paper, and plastic that you can't reuse.
- Make your own fertilizer with compost from the kitchen and your own yard.
- Organize a recycling system for your workplace, especially for office paper.
- Use recycled paper products whenever possible. Labels to look for are "post-consumer," and "unbleached."
- Print church bulletins on recycled paper—and collect them at the door for recycling.
- Recycle automotive effluent: motor oil, air-conditioning coolant, tires, batteries—even the old body itself.

MEDITATION

Autumn and the Fall

What we call the beginning is often the end
And to make an end is to make a beginning.
The end is where we start from.
　　　　　—T.S. Eliot, "Little Gidding"

૪ન

OUR WHOLE CULTURE gears up in the fall for beginnings. Business, family, church, school—all are ready in the autumn to begin new programs and projects. So the fall of the year is perhaps the best place to break into the circle of the seasons and begin considering specific things we can do to care for creation.

But autumn is also a kind of end. Children may be most aware of this: however much they might look forward to new things, they know that the endless days of summer are over. Autumn is one of our most vivid reminders that creation moves in cycles.

For autumn is the time of harvest. Most of us live too far from fields and orchards to experience that harvest directly, but even in the heart of the city we are aware of at least one inconvenient harvest fact: in eating the fruit or vegetable we throw away a great deal. Some of this is inevitable: fruits have inedible cores, carrots and potatoes have skins, lettuce has wilted leaves, and nuts have shells. About eleven percent of residential garbage is made up of such waste. But almost as much (nine percent) is made up of edible items. So although harvest brings a stream of good things into our stores, kitchens, and stomachs, it is offset by a stream of waste flowing back into creation.

This immediate waste from (and of) our food is only a tiny part of this stream. When we add to it the fuel and fertilizer needed to grow crops; the energy needed to harvest, process, and transport them; the glass, plastic, metal, and paper with which we package and promote them, it becomes obvious that harvest, which is the source of our food, is the end of a great many other things. Many of the problems we are trying to speak to in this book come from our waste. But when we think about "throwing things away," it becomes obvious how our language has trapped us. For that there is no "away" is a basic ecological law.

Harvest draws on the cycles of the earth for our nourishment, but in much of our activity that circle is broken. The fall of the year, this time of beginnings and of endings, can remind us of our broken relation to creation.

And it should remind us of another Fall. Some of the waste that we produce is an inevitable part of being a creature: it is not in itself sinful. Organic creation involves eating, digesting, excreting, even dying. This is the earth God made. The evil, rather, comes from attitudes of selfishness, carelessness, short-sightedness from sin.

We are not used to thinking of the health of the earth as a consequence of our fallenness; nevertheless, the connection between righteousness and the health of the land is a frequent theme in the Old Testament, where the relationship between God's people and the land was central. Consider Hosea's words:

> Hear the word of the Lord, you Israelites, because the Lord has a charge to bring against you who live in the land: "There is no faithfulness, no love, no acknowledgment of God in the land. There is only cursing, lying and murder, stealing and adultery; they break all bounds, and bloodshed follows bloodshed. Because of this the land mourns, and all who live in it waste away; the beasts of the field and the birds of the air and the fish of the sea are dying."
> —Hosea 4:1-3

How Fallen Is Nature?

One common attitude toward the created world gets in the way of any serious stewardship of it. That is the conviction that it is fallen. The natural order of eating, nutrition, excrement, dying, and decay—all those cycles which keep the world balanced—are often regarded as the result of sin. Christians have sometimes felt that since nature is a tapestry of suffering and pain, it cannot be the world God called good. Therefore some have concluded that our responsibility for such a creation should not be to perpetuate it, but to shape it back to God's purpose through a reasserted dominion. Many even declare that since eventually God will create a new earth, we should not be overly concerned about this one.

This idea is a misinterpretation of Genesis 3, where God says to Adam, "Cursed is the ground because of you; through painful toil you will eat of it all the days of your life. It will produce thorns and thistles for you." This has been interpreted as meaning that God's good creation had no thorns, thistles, carnivorosity, or death, that it was a soft world without painful conflict. But a closer look at this passage suggests not that thorns, thistles, and the necessity of eating sprang into being at the instant of human sin, but that human sin sets us *against* creation in such a way that these things become a curse. (The passage could read, "Cursed is the ground *to you.*") The problem is one of human relationship: a broken relationship with the Creator leads to a broken relationship to creation. Conversely, a healed relationship with God leads to a healed relationship with creation. As Paul wrote, "If anyone is in Christ, there is a new creation" (2 Cor 5:17).

Hosea was not speaking of the way the land mourns today (in clear-cut forests, or erosive agriculture, or the ozone-destroying accumulation of gasses in the upper atmosphere). We cannot be certain of the particular situation he was describing. But the principle is clear: the effects of human sin are not confined to individual men and women. Like the casting of a heavy stone, its ripples spread through all of creation and leave nothing untouched.

Our fallenness is particularly evident in the habits by which we treat the rest of creation as an endless stock-pile—or an endless waste heap. We are all in a hurry to be about our own business, which traps us into ignoring the Creator's business—and the needs and health of creation.

So in the fall of the year, as we enjoy creation's harvest and begin our own individual projects, it is good to think about two kinds of "fall." One is the created autumn in which fruits ripen, gardens wither, and seeds fall into the ground and die. The celebration of Thanksgiving is a good way to recall those created gifts that are both an end and a beginning. But we need to remember as well, in repentance, a second kind of fall: the fall which we enact daily in our selfishness, which makes us treat creation as though it were only our tool or toy, good only for our convenience.

Here it is helpful to remember the beginning of the church year, Advent. In our culture we have become so enamored with the feast of Christmas that we forget the long waiting for the Messiah that characterized Judaism and that should still characterize our anticipation of the second coming of Christ. Thus we may forget that Advent is not only the herald of Christmas: it is, in the darkening days of autumn, a penitential season, an occasion for self-examination and self-discipline. And nowhere is that discipline needed more than in our use and misuse of creation. Caring for creation is a matter of habit, and our habits need changing.

The Anglican Collect for Advent is oddly appropriate for

this determined effort to change the habits by which we throw things away. For it invokes God's help in the "casting away" of old habits themselves:

Almighty God, give us grace that we may cast away the works of darkness, and put upon us the armor of light, now in the time of this mortal life, in which thy Son Jesus Christ came to visit us in great humility.

—*The Book of Common Prayer*

❧ ONE ❧

Reduce

Watch out! Be on your guard against all kinds of greed; a man's life does not consist of the abundance of his possessions.

—Luke 12:15

In many ways, we might be happier with less. In the final analysis, accepting and living by sufficiency rather than excess offers a return to what is, culturally speaking, the human home: to the ancient order of family, community, good work, and good life; to a reverence for excellence of skilled handiwork; to a true materialism that does not just care about *things but cares* for *them; to communities worth spending a lifetime in.*

—Alan Durning, "Asking How Much Is Enough," *State of the World*

❧

CHRISTIANS SHOULD NEVER say that the use of creation is fundamentally wrong, that the less one uses the more righteous he or she is. That is a gnostic idea, based on the premise that the physical world is an illusion. No, creation is good, and good for us, and we ought to delight in its use.

But it is all too easy for us to think that creation is exclusively and inexhaustibly for our consumption. So we need to know how to *fast* as well as feast, and that is a harder lesson. Blinded by a civilization that has for a long time been able to produce more and more things at a lower and lower cost, it is easy for us to forget the limits of creation. So we need to learn moderation: we need to unlearn habits of thoughtless consumption and waste. We need, in short, to live in ways that *reduce* the damage we do to creation.

In this chapter we give some advice about reducing our use of energy, water, packaging, and toxic materials. The first two things are gifts from God, valuable in their own right. We reduce our use in order to cherish them. The second two are human products, of limited value, and we reduce our use of them to keep from injuring God's creation.

A Family Story

Till I was about twelve years old my mother cooked on a wood-burning stove, which also (through coils in the firebox) heated our hot water. It seemed like a good arrangement to me: I remember with pleasure the warm space between the wall and the stove, close by the crackle of dry fir and maple firewood. But then I wasn't responsible for starting the fire in the morning, keeping it going through the day—or, even in the heat of summer, cooking and canning over a hot block of iron. So I can appreciate my mother's delight when we could finally afford an electric stove—and an electric water heater.

Electricity was cheap then, and we were one of the only families around who still cooked on wood. So, with great relief, we welcomed the gleaming white appliances into the kitchen and entered the push-button convenience of the twentieth century.

Twenty years earlier, when my parents got married, they camped for their honeymoon in a moss-draped old forest along the McKenzie River, a tributary of the Willamette in Oregon's Cascade Mountains. They carved a heart deep in the grey bark of an old alder and cut their names inside. When their first child was born, they returned and added his initials to the heart; five years later they added the initials of my sister; five years more and my initials joined the others on the alder bark, while the cold, green river poured on past the ancient trees.

But in another five years, when my younger brother was born, the honeymoon tree was gone, and so was the river. The population of the Willamette Valley was growing, and as it grew so did its insatiable demand for cheap electricity. And what better way to generate the electricity than to channel the inexhaustible flow of the mountain rivers through turbines at the foot of dams?

In those days of seemingly endless valleys and forests, few mourned a cut tree. My mother mourned the loss of the honeymoon tree; my father, a logger at heart, made fun of her soft-heartedness. But neither noticed the inexorable connection between the gleaming, silent servants in the kitchen and the disappearance of the riverside alder that recorded our family's growth.

Was it wrong to build the dam that flooded the valley in order to generate the electricity that powered my mother's new stove? Should we all go back to cooking on wood today? The answer is clearly "no" to both questions. There are few better ways of generating electricity than using the force of falling water. And if everyone cooked with wood, the pollution and deforestation problems would be extreme.

If there is anything to be learned from this sad story of the new stove and the honeymoon tree, it is that all of our conveniences have their price, usually a price paid by mute creation. We who would be the Creator's stewards need to know that price and do all we can to make it less.

ENERGY

Energy is the most basic of creation's resources, for it is only through using energy that we can use anything else. In an Edenic existence where all we had to do was pick fruits and vegetables to eat, we would use only the amount of energy produced in our bodies by the food we eat: about 2500 calories. But few (if any) can live so simple a life. Very early we learned to harness the energy of animals. Later, but still a long time ago, we tapped into the cycles of creation by harnessing wind and water. Much more recently—in the eighteenth century—we began to burn coal, then oil and natural gas. Today North Americans on the average use about 250,000 calories of energy each day, giving us each the equivalent of a hundred slaves.

The problem is not the relative luxury this energy gives us. It is rather that the waste products of obtaining, transporting, and burning the fuels that produce the energy degrade creation. For God's earth runs on solar energy. The daily income of the sun's heat moves its air and waters. The photosynthesis of plants makes the sun's light available to us as food and wood, and over time it accumulates in the coal, oil, and gas that we burn.

We have many practical reasons for shifting from a civilization that is burning up our fossil fuel "savings" in a century or two to a civilization that runs, as does the rest of earthly creation, on energy income: the energy of the sun. But more important even than the good political and economic reasons is our responsibility to God for the care of creation. For the manner and extent of our use of energy is doing great harm.

We cannot simply withdraw from an energy-wasteful civilization. But we can begin to change it by reducing our use. Here are some specific ways.

Heating and Cooling Homes. A large percentage of energy used in North America is consumed in heating (and in certain areas, in cooling) our homes and buildings. Here are some things you can do to reduce that drain on creation.

Stop your home from leaking heat. The methods for doing this range from the simple and cheap (like installing weather stripping around doors and windows) to the more complex and expensive (like blowing insulation between the walls). A little research will indicate what is appropriate for your home. Most new homes, thankfully, are designed and built to keep the heat in, but old houses may need a lot of work.

Learn how to be comfortable at a lower temperature. Wear a sweater or a wool shirt around the house during the day, and discover the pleasure of sleeping under heavy blankets and flannel sheets in a cool room at night. An extra quilt or two accomplishes the same thing as an electric blanket.

Plant trees for shade in summer. Deciduous trees provide shade in summer when it is needed, and they lose their leaves in the fall to admit the sun for warmth. The energy savings alone can be enormous, not to mention the other benefits of carefully placed trees. (See "Trees" section in chapter seven.)

Focus the warmth in your homes. Focus is the Latin word for "hearth," and it expresses a profound truth. Just as rays of light are bent by a lens to a hot, bright point, so also a friendly source of heat in a home draws its residents around it. This is an unabashed argument for the use of fireplaces, which have been strongly criticized as inefficient heaters. They *are* inefficient—if they are expected to heat the far corners of a house. But evening is when the members of a household ought to be drawn together, not scattered to their warm and isolated cells. And a fireplace makes a far better focus than a TV.

Appliance Use. One of the obvious ways that energy functions in our homes as a servant is in the machines that we use to heat our water, cook our food, wash and dry our clothes, keep us lighted, and so on. We need to be aware of the amount of energy these appliances use and weigh carefully whether and how much we should use them.

Energy Use in Appliances

	Average kW.h used in 2 months	2 month cost at $.05/kW.h
Refrigerating and freezing:		
Old refrigerator, 10-12 cu. ft., manual defrost	200	10.00
Energy-efficient refrigerator, 10-12 cu. ft., manual defrost	90	4.50
Old frost-free refrigerator-freezer, 17 cu. ft.	280	14.00
Energy-efficient frost-free refrigerator-freezer, 17 cu. ft.	170	8.50
Old freezer, chest, 12-16 cu. ft.	180	9.00
Energy-efficient freezer, chest, 12-16 cu. ft.	120	6.00
Old freezer, upright 16 cu. ft.	210	10.50
Energy-efficient freezer, upright 16 cu. ft.	160	8.00
Cooking:		
Electric range, manually cleaned oven	130	6.50
Self-cleaning oven, 1 cleaning/mo.	138	6.90
Microwave oven, 30 min./day	40	2.00
Electric frying pan, 15 times/mo.	24	1.20
Coffee maker, 50 times/mo.	24	1.20
Toaster oven, 15 times/mo.	23	1.15
Dishwasher, not including hot water:		
Using dry cycle, 1 time/day	36	1.80
Without dry cycle, 1 time/day	20	1.00
Laundry:		
Dryer, 1 load/day	160	8.00
Washer, 1 load/day, not including hot water	16	.80
Iron, 2 hr./week	8	.40
Lighting, lit 5 hr./day, providing equal light:		
4 100-watt incandescent lamps	122	6.10
2 40-watt fluorescent lamps	28	1.40
Entertainment:		
Color TV, 6 hr./day	70	3.50
Stereo, 3 hr./day	22	1.10
Radio, 3 hr./day	14	.70
Personal Comfort:		
Waterbed, any size	200	10.00
Portable space heater, 1000 watts	180	9.00
Electric blanket, double size	20	1.20
Electric Water Heating, average for a family of 4:		
Standard water heater	950	47.00
Energy-efficient electric water heater	900	45.00

BC hydro August 1991

When thinking about the energy we use in home appliances, keep two principles in mind.

First, by far the heaviest energy users are appliances whose purpose is to heat or cool. Thus cookstoves, water heaters, refrigerators, and electric dryers come near the top of the list. Appliances with electric motors (like vacuum cleaners and food processors) use relatively little energy, though you still have to consider the energy expended in their manufacture.

Second, be aware that the real cost of purchasing any appliance—even a light bulb—is the purchase price plus the energy costs of that appliance across its lifetime. In many cases the cheapest alternative in the long run is the most expensive initially.

Here are some specific things you can do to reduce the costs to creation of your appliance-servants:

Buy the most energy-efficient appliance. It may cost more, but will, in the long run, treat creation more gently.

The eyes open to a cry of pulleys....
Outside the open window
The morning air is all awash with angels.

Some are in bed-sheets, some are in blouses,
Some are in smocks: but truly there they are....
'O, let there be nothing on earth but laundry,
Nothing but rosy hands in the rising steam
And clear dances done in the sight of heaven.'
— Richard Wilbur,
"Love Calls Us to the Things of This World"

Shift from clothes-dryer to clothesline. This sounds laborious, but it isn't. And there are some real advantages: the scent of clothes hung in the sun and the wind is vastly better than clothes from a dryer. And being dependent on the sun for drying makes you more aware of the sky, the clouds, the weather, the progression of shadows through the day and the seasons. It's a way of making you more aware of your life as a creature. And there are few jobs more relaxing (or satisfying) than hanging up—and taking down—clothes from a clothesline.

Of course not everyone can have an outdoor clothesline, and there are several months of the year that resist outdoor drying. But folding wooden clothes racks are cheap and easily stored. Hang clothes up in the evening and they're almost always dry by morning. And during the night they've restored to your house some of the moisture that winter heating removes.

> *Sing hey! for the bath at close of day*
> *that washes the weary mud away!*
> *A loon is he who will not sing:*
> *O! Water Hot is a noble thing!*
> —J.R.R. Tolkien,
> *The Fellowship of the Ring*

Use and heat your hot water less wastefully. Hot water is a great luxury—as this scrap of song from a weary hobbit in Tolkien's *The Fellowship of the Ring* makes clear. But we no longer (like the hobbits) heat it kettle by kettle on the stove: we want (and have) it abundant and inexhaustible. It's no surprise then that hot water is one of the highest energy users in the home. But there are many ways to have it available more cheaply.

Turn down the setting on your hot water tank. The low setting (about 115 degrees) is enough for most home uses. And turn off the water heater entirely if you're going to be gone for more than a few days.

Insulate your tank and the hot water lines leading from it.

Save baths for very special occasions: they use a lot more water and energy than showers. (Unless you take *very* long showers. Some people—notably teen-agers—consider the shower an alternate environment, something to *live* in!)

Install "low-flow" shower heads that mix air and water, maintaining pressure for a pleasant shower but using considerably less water. Buy the kind that turns off at the shower head, and turn it off while soaping up. (Low-flow heads will pay for themselves in a few months.)

If you're building a house or replacing a water heater, consider some alternate systems: "demand heaters" have no storage tank, but use a high-power heat source to produce a steady stream of hot water only when it is needed. (They are common in more frugal parts of the world like Europe and Japan.) Since the steady heat-leakage from the storage tank is avoided, they save about a quarter of your water-heating costs. A solar water heater is a proven technology, even for cloudy areas. Over a million homes in the United States have them, and in some Mediterranean countries they produce over half of the hot water. For a guaranteed supply, a solar heater should be used as a preheater for another system (though it's not a bad creaturely discipline to adjust periods of high hot-water use to periods of high sunshine). Solar systems are expensive to install but cheap to operate. And you feel cleaned by more than the water when taking a sun-heated shower: you're using the God-given gift of creativity to wisely steward the equally God-given water and sunlight.

Two excellent little books (free!) on energy use in the home are *Saving Energy and Money with Home Appliances* and *The Most Energy-Efficient Appliances*, produced by The American Council for an Energy-Efficient Economy, Suite 535, 1001 Connecticut Avenue, NW, Washington, DC 20036.

Lighting. The Bible describes the making of light as the first of God's creative acts. Light is such an obvious good that we use it as a synonym for good, and its absence, dark, as a word for evil. So we speak of the "dawning of an era" or "the light of civilization." And as our skill has allowed it, we increasingly surround ourselves with light.

Yet light is a form of energy: to waste it is to waste energy and degrade creation. So we need to learn to cherish light, to use and produce it wisely. Here are some simple ways:

Don't light areas needlessly. Turn off the lights when they're not being used. And don't overlight areas, like hallways, which don't need it.

Switch to fluorescent lights. It's now possible to buy fluorescent fixtures that screw into a socket that normally holds an incandescent bulb. These are expensive—$15 to $30 per bulb—but they use only a quarter of the energy and last up to ten times as long as a regular bulb. The light is steady and warm, not the flickering white that has made fluorescents unattractive for homes and hard on the eyes.

This single change could save a great deal of energy use and money. Jon Luoma, a writer for *Audubon,* has calculated that, "If, say, two-thirds of the three billion incandescent sockets in America were relamped with compact fluorescents, the economy would save some $20 billion annually, and [the equivalent of] 250 million barrels of oil."[1]

Learn to cherish light by developing an appreciation for darkness. Or at least, for less light. Some of God's greatest gifts are evident only in a darkness that is increasingly rare. Many urban children have never seen the stars, for example. We need to learn the pleasures of candlelight, of firelight, of starlight— and of the pool of light that floods the area where we need it but leaves depth and shadow outside. We have probably grown too used to uniform bright light, and thus have lost appreciation for the range of light and dark that is part of God's earth.

Transportation. Of all our uses of energy, perhaps the greatest room for reduction is in our transportation. Since the invention of the internal combustion engine and the availability of relatively cheap cars and gasoline, North America

The deadly power of rushing about wherever I pleased had not been given me. I measured distance by the standard of man, man walking on his two feet, not by the standard of the internal combustion engine.... The truest and most horrible claim made for modern transport is that it "annihilates space." It does. It annihilates one of the most glorious gifts we have been given. It is a vile inflation which lowers the value of distance, so that a modern boy travels a hundred miles with less sense of liberation and pilgrimage and adventure than his grandfather got from traveling ten. Of course if a man hates space and wants it annihilated, that is another matter. Why not creep into his coffin at once? There is little enough space there.

— C.S. Lewis, *Surprised by Joy*
(New York: Harcourt, Brace and Company, 1955),

has built a way of life dependent on the automobile. Though the immediate appeal of this mobility is evident, the overall result—for the whole earth, and for human communities in particular—has been disastrous. (See chapter eleven for more details on the impact of cars on creation.)

Here are some simple and obvious things *you* can do to begin to detach from our automotive culture.

Walk or ride a bike. We're used to getting in the car to travel distances earlier generations walked with ease. Usually we say we don't have time to walk. But since we also spend more time and money on recreation and exercise than any other people, that argument is not always persuasive. We Christians claim a personal relationship with the master of the universe, but we insulate ourselves from that universe in our enclosed wheeled worlds. Walking or biking slows our life down, opens all our senses up to God's creation, makes us accessible to other creatures, strengthens our bodies—and reduces the amount of oil we burn, the amount of waste we put into the atmosphere.

Use public transportation. Of course we can't walk everywhere. But buses and trains provide a good way for us to go places with much less cost to creation. Planes, unfortunately, are worse than cars in their per-passenger-mile energy consumption. Trains, on the other hand, are one of the most efficient ways of travel. Many people disdain buses as low-class and trains as too slow, so that governments put more and more money into road systems and dismantle their passenger trains.

Save gas in the way you drive. Gradual acceleration and deceleration uses less gas than fast stops and starts. And as speeds rise above 55-60 MPH, fuel efficiency declines dramatically.

Energy Intensity of Transport Modes

Mode	Energy Intensity Calories per passenger kilometer
Automobile, 1 occupant	1,143
Transit Bus	570
Transit Rail	549
Walking	62
Bicycling	22

Marcia D. Lowe, "Cycling into the Future," Lester Brown, ed., *State of the World 1990* (New York: W.W. Norton & Co., 1990), 124.

The Rocky Mountain Institute (1729 Snowmass Creek Road, Snowmass, CO 81654-9199) is an excellent resource for information about our energy use and about ways to change wasteful habits, both individually and nationally.

WATER

Water in the Bible is often presented as a gift of God: the stream that gushed from the rock in the wilderness of Sinai; the rain that came after Elijah's prayer; the many places in the Psalms where God is described as the one who "supplies the earth with rain." And Jesus tells a woman drawing water of the water he gives, "welling up to eternal life" (see Jn 4:7-15). Several of Jesus' miracles involve water. But water itself is a kind of miracle. The only substance on the planet that naturally occurs in solid, liquid, and gaseous state, it is essential to all living things.

Like many of creation's gifts, we have removed ourselves so far from the source and the destination of the water we use that we find it easy to take for granted. But even when we do think about water, the facts seem encouraging. The amount of water on the planet is enormous—326 million cubic miles. It is also constant; and because it cycles from ocean to air to the ground, through rivers and into oceans again, we might think that it can never be in short supply. But as many communities around the world have discovered—and are discovering—water is often not there when and where we need it. Of all that water, only three percent is fresh, and two-thirds of that is ice. Of the remaining one percent, half is in the ground and most of the rest is in the air. So only about 1/5000th of the earth's water is fresh in lakes and streams, and much of that is polluted. (We will have more to say in chapter twelve about water *quality*—for now we're concerned with the *quantity* of good water.)

In many areas of the world, fresh water is in drastically short supply. If you live in the American southwest, for example, where we have built a kind of urban desert society dependent on imported water, you are acutely aware of water needs. For most of us the situation is not as crucial: the water flows from the tap when we want it, and down our drains and toilets when we're through. But to make it so readily available to our steadily growing demands we build dams, reservoirs, canals, and tunnels, flooding valleys or draining marshes, diminishing creation's richness.

Much of our per-person water use is accounted for in agriculture (it takes more than one hundred gallons to grow enough wheat for a loaf of bread) and in industry (it takes about 250 *tons* of water to make a ton of steel—or a ton of paper). We can indirectly begin to affect that use through what we eat and buy. But a great deal of water usage is in the home. One researcher has estimated that a family of four at home for a day in the summer is likely to use 120 gallons flushing the toilet, 24 gallons brushing teeth, 167 gallons bathing, 660 gallons watering the lawn, and so on. All the uses adding up to over 1200 gallons.[2]

So here are a few simple things you can do to conserve this created gift of water.

Watch Your Habits while Showering, Shaving, and Brushing Your Teeth. Shorten the amount of time the water runs during these activities. The best way by far is to turn the water off when you're not using it—while soaping, shaving, brushing. Then turn it on again when you need to rinse. (See previous "Energy" section for information on low-flow showerheads, which make it easier to turn off the water in mid-shower.)

Give Your Home a "Water Audit," Looking for Leaks. Then fix the leaks, calling in a plumber if necessary. The results can be spectacular. The average toilet leaks up to 100 gallons per day; a toilet has to leak about 250 gallons per day before you can even *hear* the leak. Put dye in your tank and see if it seeps into the bowl. Even a slow faucet drip can amount to many gallons of water in a month.

Install Water-saving Devices. Two are particularly helpful. One is the low-flow shower head described previously. And you can buy a "toilet dam," a plastic gadget that divides your toilet tank into three compartments, only one of which flushes, thus saving about three gallons per flush. Alternatively, put a plastic bottle filled with water in the tank: the water displaced will be saved at each flush. Or try the even lower-tech solution of discouraging flushing after each use. We've posted this "Galiano maxim" (named for the water-poor island where we live) by our toilets: "When it's yellow, let it mellow; When it's brown, flush it down!"

Water Lawns Less. Green lawns are undeniably pleasant and beautiful. But—especially in dry periods and places—they are unacceptably thirsty. You might consider reducing their size or making them edible (see chapter seven, "Planting"). Another answer to the problem of water-hungry lawns is the growing art of xeriscaping (from *xeros*, the Greek word for dry): landscaping with plants that use little water.

PACKAGING

In our quest for convenience we use up more and more of creation as a one-time container for things. Thirty percent of our garbage (by weight) and fifty percent (by volume) is packaging. Over ten percent of America's aluminum, fifty percent of its paper, and fully ninety percent of its glass goes into packaging. Almost all of this is used once and thrown away. These facts ought to make us question whether this is a good way to care for creation. It certainly is not a very good way to run a civilization.

We're constantly tempted into seeing the amount and expense of packaging as a measure of worth. But quality is not measured by packaging. In fact, packaging in the store is a regular Pandora's box of costs to creation. Here are the hidden costs of a box of rice—from tree to cooking pot:

—Trees cut down to make boxes
Cost: potential erosion, destruction of wildlife habitat, use of fuel, increase of carbon dioxide in the atmosphere
—Transportation of trees to processing plant
Cost: fuel, air pollution
—Transforming wood to pulp, pulp to paper, and paper to box
Cost: fuel, air, and water pollution (If the box is from recycled materials, these will be reduced.)
—Transportation of box to packaging plant
Cost: fuel, air pollution
—Transportation of packaged rice to store
Cost: fuel—more than transmitting bulk rice, because of the weight of the packaging, and because the rice settles till the boxes are only three-fourths full.

So when we buy our rice in a box, the cost of the rice reflects only a small percentage of the total cost.

Once we have eaten the rice, the adventures (and costs) of the rice box go on:

—Box discarded in garbage
Cost: our energy—about equal to putting a jar of rice back on the shelf.
—Box transported to landfill, incinerator, or recycling center.
Cost: in the dump or landfill the box will take decades to decompose.

The glass jar we could have used for bulk rice has a longer—but less interesting—life span. It's limited to short trips off the shelf for refill. The hidden cost to its maker and you: the initial cost of making the jar, a little handling, and an occasional cleaning. If you don't drop it (always a possibility), it could last for centuries. If you do drop it, the glass is easily recycled.

We need to get in the habit of looking in this way at every container. Our excessive packaging, in the long run, makes food more expensive. So a critical look at the package can, in the long run, be a reminder to value the heart of the matter—in this case, the rice, which is all we really wanted.

Here are some starters for reducing the volume of packaging in our municipal waste from fifty percent to zero.

Buy in Bulk. But be careful; storing up for tomorrow may mean yet more waste. Ask yourself these questions:

Do I have a good place to store it?

Will it spoil before I use it? Will I ever really use this much?

How much will fit in my storage container?

Choose Containers Carefully. If possible, choose from the beginning of the following list, not the end.

1. Refillable is better than recyclable. *Glass* milk and beverage bottles can actually be used again and again.
2. Recyclable glass is better than recyclable steel or aluminum.
3. Recycled containers are better than first-use containers. Look for the "Recycled" sign. If a box is grey (instead of white) on the inside, that means that it's made from recycled materials. Paper that is recycled *and* unbleached is best.
4. Recyclable containers are better than nonrecyclable containers.
5. Recyclable plastics. Buy as a last resort. Check to see if they really *can* be recycled in your area.
6. Biodegradable is better than nonbiodegradable.
7. Avoid foil-lined boxes or bags. They can't be recycled or re-used.

See "Energy Consumption Per Use for 12-oz. Beverage Containers" on page 46.

Energy Consumption Per Use for 12-Ounce Beverage Containers

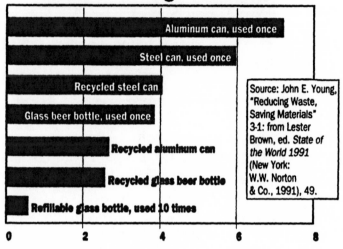

Aluminum can, used once

Steel can, used once

Recycled steel can

Glass beer bottle, used once

Recycled aluminum can

Recycled glass beer bottle

Refillable glass bottle, used 10 times

0   2   4   6   8

Source: John E. Young, "Reducing Waste, Saving Materials" 3-1: from Lester Brown, ed. *State of the World 1991* (New York: W.W. Norton & Co., 1991), 49.

The packaging industry has begun to respond to criticisms, which is good news. What's bad news is that the response is often to continue making the offending product but (through clever advertising and labeling) to try to convince potential buyers that *this* package is at least "good for the environment" or "biodegradable" or "earth-friendly." Sometimes the claims are true; often, sadly, they are misleading or downright false. Read *all* advertising with considerable skepticism, especially advertising about the environmental friendliness of throwaway packaging.

Stow away your own shopping container. Keep a box in your car with your own packaging in it:

—An assortment of clean plastic bags for bulk purchases.
—Some sturdy reusable shopping bags.

—Some newspaper for cushioning fragile items.

The box is important: it will keep your packaging from disintegrating into car rubbish.

Carry a net or cloth bag with you whenever possible, or use your purse or pocket for small purchases. Avoid a whole collection of itty-bitty bags from single purchases of such things as candybars and cards. (Some stores take a dim view of unbagged objects in pockets and purses. Be sure to keep your receipt for purchase proof!)

Be polite and considerate in refusing bags. We don't want to save a bag and lose a battle.

For more information: write to Pennsylvania Resources Council, 25 West Third Street, P.O. Box 88, Media, PA 19063, or call 1-800-GO-TO-PRC. This group publishes guidelines called *Become an Environmental Shopper,* a preferred product list, and an *Environmental Shopping Update,* which comes out twice a year.

DON'T JUST REDUCE, REFUSE

> *"... give me neither poverty nor riches,*
> *but give me only my daily bread.*
> *Otherwise, I may have too much and disown you*
> *and say, 'Who is the Lord?'*
> *Or I may become poor and steal,*
> *and so dishonor the name of my God."*
> —Proverbs 30:8-9

ða

"All the worry over ecology fails to stem consumption," declares a recent headline. In the last three sections we discussed ways to reduce that consumption. Sometimes, however, we need to do more than Reduce, we need to downright Refuse. We can say "No." "Just say No" is a slogan widely used in the campaign to eliminate drug abuse. "Consumerism" can be like drug abuse: we buy and consume products to make us feel better for a little while. The best defense is to "Just Say No."

Cut Consumption: The Four Spending Laws of the Conscientious Consumer.

Battle with bargains you don't really need. Try want-ads, freight-damage stores, or anything that isn't retail. Checkout counter bargains are, of course, absolute no-nos. They appeal to a human inability to "just say no" which is as old as Adam.

Wage war on whims. Take a shopping list based on well-thought-out needs. If you see something that you didn't realize you needed, but that you've always wanted, and know you'll really use, think again. Better yet, go home and think about it. A good part of the time you'll forget about your whim or even realize with horror your close brush with foolishness.

Banish browse buying. Shopping may be just an expensive cure for boredom. Malls are not places for taking vacations or field trips. For an outing, try a place where there's not so much for sale—like a park or a museum.

Hold out against hidden persuaders. We all need to be aware of the powerful persuasion in ads, especially TV ads where the double whammy of sight and sound can exert subliminal sexual and emotional appeals that are difficult to resist. Throwing away your TV is probably the best defense!

For some help at resisting advertising and consumerism, get in touch with *Adbusters*, a quarterly magazine published by a group which prepares alternative "anti-ad" TV commercials. Write to THE MEDIA FOUNDATION, 1243 West 7th Avenue, Vancouver, BC, Canada, V6H 1B7, or call 604-736-9401.

Choose Caring for Creation over Personal Convenience.
God didn't make a throwaway world. But we make—and

use—many throwaway things out of what he made. The throwaway, plastic versions of razors, pens, pencils, diapers, and cameras are prime examples. Some of these are technically recyclable, but their components are not going to be separated enough for efficient recycling.

We need to resist not only this "throwaway" tendency, but also a "gadget-happy" streak, which comes out in the shop, the garden, the car, but most often the kitchen. These gadgets are often good for only one job—a job that can be done equally well by a hand tool or machine in a little more time. If these gadgets break down, the repair job is usually at least as expensive as the replacement. Often the gadget is made in such a way that makes repair impossible. Buy the gadget the way you would choose any helper: pick something that can do more than one job, and which will last a long time.

Some sample one-job electrical helpers to reconsider are electric can openers, yogurt makers, popcorn makers, hand mixers (which can, of course, mix many things, but often bog down in the sort of mixing we need help with), electric ice cream mixers, and bread machines.

Some sample substitutes are hand-operated can openers (the kind with a decent grip), egg beaters, wire whips, ordinary pots, pans, and bowls. These are all excellent, multipurpose kitchen aids. We're not advocating giving up on electrical gadgets—rather suggesting that we learn to get by with a few genuinely multi-purpose ones.

TOXINS

Toxin means "poison." We've heard a lot recently about "toxic wastes," but we would be mistaken if we thought that it was only government and industries that had to deal with poisonous substances. We regularly use poisons to wash our clothes, clean our stoves, kill our pests, and manage our gardens. They're often dangerous to use—and always dangerous to dispose of. It would be better to "just say no" to such household poisons, and find alternative ways of doing the job. But first use up what you have at home and carefully dispose of the container. The toxins we're going to look at in this section are the ones most commonly used.

Pesticides. Look up your problem in a reliable garden book and find a safe solution. In caring for your pets follow this regimen:

—a weekly bath in gentle soap
—a weekly powder with rotenone (a harmless and edible garden and pet insecticide)
—frequent vacuuming of rugs during flea season
—a flea-collar of cotton clothesline saturated with mint oil or extract; to renew just re-oil (only needed during peak flea seasons)
—a bed sprinkled or stuffed with cedar chips

Aerosols. Spray-can aerosols have a nasty reputation for being unfriendly to creation. The reputation is deserved. Here's why:

1. Aerosols may contain chlorinated fluorocarbons (CFC's), which are one of the main causes for depletion of the ozone layer. (Though some spray cans advertise their innocence, most CFC substitutes have their own problems. Better to avoid aerosol sprays entirely.)

2. Due to their explosive potential even when supposedly empty, and their plastic component, aerosol cans are not easily recyclable.

3. The fine spray of aerosols sends tiny droplets into the air, resulting both in waste and (often) real danger from breathing the suspended leftovers.

In short, say No to aerosol cans: it's a convenience we can forego, and creation will be healthier for it.

Non-rechargeable Batteries. These are difficult to recycle unless they are sorted into like types. The possibility that they can be recycled (or perhaps, eventually, recharged) is a comfort to those of us—like the hard of hearing—who depend on them. Use solar-powered alternatives (or solar rechargers) wherever possible. They are steadily becoming cheaper and more available. (For information on solar-powered alternatives, see "Real Goods" below.)

Bleached Non-recycled Paper Products. Avoid these whenever possible. See the section "Recycle Paper Waste" in chapter three for facts and figures on Dioxins and first-use paper.

Cleaning Culprits. Here's a chance to cut down on both toxins and containers. Copy the following pages of clean cleaners and clean cleaning combinations and tape it inside a closet or cupboard door for easy reference.

Clean cleaners. Keep these in the house at all times:

—Baking soda: deodorizer, cleaner, and fire extinguisher!
—White vinegar: solvent and softener
—Plain old soap (such as Ivory Flakes or homemade soap)
—Washing soda: cleaner and deodorizer
—Borax: bleach and sanitizer (use sparingly)
—Ammonia: a strong cleaner (use sparingly)

Real Goods

An excellent source for creation-friendly products is Real Goods, 966 Mazzoni Street, Ukiah, CA 95482 (707-468-9214), which describes itself as "the largest selection of alternative energy products for a cleaner and safer world." In addition to a general catalogue, Real Goods has for subscribers an annual alternative energy sourcebook, a 400-page energy encyclopedia packed with up-to-date information on less wasteful ways of using energy.

Clean cleaning combinations. Here are some common household cleaning supplies:

— General cleaner: 1 part baking soda or washing soda to 8 parts water. If the job needs a stronger treatment, add 1 part vinegar or even 1 part borax.
— Dish detergent: 2 cups soap flakes to 4 quarts water.
— Dishwasher detergent: use one with no phosphates, or make your own mix with 2 parts borax and 1 part baking soda.
— Laundry detergent: plain soap flakes and washing soda. (We find that 2/3 cup Ivory Flakes and 1/3 cup washing soda work very well.) Put these into the washer before the clothes. Use Calgon every so often to take out soap residues, or add 1/3 cup washing soda with the soap flakes and 1/2 cup borax as needed for whitening. Add 1/2 cup vinegar to the rinse for a softener (and for the final rinse of diapers to neutralize urine). Whites, however, to stay white may need an occasional heavy-duty treatment by bleach or detergents.
— Oven cleaner: clean up spills immediately, and save toxins and scrubbing! Moisten surface, sprinkle on baking soda and salt. Wait a few minutes (especially if the spill is greasy) and wipe off. You may have to resort to steel wool or a "Mr. Muscle" workout, after which you make a New Year's Oven Resolution.
— Disinfectant: 1/2 cup borax dissolved in 1 quart water.
— Toilet bowl cleaner: baking soda. For sediment buildup, add a generous dose of vinegar and let fizz for a while.
— Bleach: try borax for general brightening. As an alternative to weekly bleaching of whites, buy dark things that won't need bleaching: for example, dark dish cloths, dish towels, hand towels, and underwear.
— Window cleaner: put 2 tablespoons vinegar in your own 1 quart spray container and fill up with water.

—Copper cleaner: cover copper piece with paste of vinegar, salt, and cornstarch. Let it sit for a few minutes.

—Silver cleaner: cover piece with salted water in an aluminum pan or foil pie tin. (The resulting electrolysis is astonishingly quick and effective.)

—Drain cleaner: the best cleaner is the user; keep grease and bits of food out of the drain. If the drain is clogged, try several spoonfuls of baking soda (or better yet, washing soda) followed by about 1/2 cup of vinegar. Wait till the fizzing stops, and finish off with a kettle of boiling water.

—Air freshener: a saucer or two of white vinegar will do wonders.

—Moth balls: use cedar chips or shavings. Make them yourself—out of an untreated red cedar or juniper board. Sprinkle lavender flowers and leaves in the bottom of the drawers, or put them in a sachet.

—Starch: 2 tablespoons cornstarch in a 1 quart spray bottle, and fill up with water.

—Furniture polish: for most furniture a non-linty rag *lightly* dampened in warm water works fine. For polished furniture, use a mixture of 1 part lemon juice to 2 parts oil (regular vegetable oil works fine).

Reuse

The world is too much with us; late and soon,
Getting and spending, we lay waste our powers....
—William Wordsworth

governing

AFTER REDUCING—OR REFUSING—the uses of creation that damage it, there are many things that we can reuse instead of throwing "away." But because reusing something—whether it's a piece of paper, a bottle, or an old board—takes a bit more effort (to remove the nails, to wash the bottle), we often just discard it. Following are four areas where we can begin instead to practice more careful use of creation through reuse.

REUSE PAPER

For some of us, paper seems to run our lives. We're surrounded by piles labeled "Take Care of Right Away," "To Be Sorted," "To Be Filed," "Letters to Answer," "Memoirs," and so on. Paper is at the heart of organization, communication, education—and garbage. Paper is the single largest component of garbage, making up almost half the content of landfills. And the demand for pulp for paper is one of the main engines of deforestation.

We *could* recycle most of what we throw away. But here the *order* of "reduce, reuse, recycle" is important. It's most important to reduce the number of things we use, thus cutting out the cost to creation of the initial production: a cost in energy, materials, and pollution. Then we need to reuse what we've had to use. Only as a last resort do we recycle. The goal is always zero garbage: to throw nothing into that non-existent place, "away."

Using paper completely is the best way to reduce paper consumption. Here is a list of some paper products we usually buy brand new, with suggestions for "used paper" substitutes. Reduce the new by reuse of the old.

Sheets of Paper. Save all paper used only on one side and use it for scratch paper and kids' drawing paper. Stapling or gluing it together in pads makes reuse easier.

Photocopiers have made it easy to waste paper. But most of the newer machines make it possible to save paper as well. Photocopy on both sides; more and more machines make this easy for you. Also you can "shrink" copy so that two pages go side-by-side. Doing this and using both sides can reduce your paper use by seventy-five percent!

You can entertain fellow committee members with a "Paper Score": the number of sheets of paper used for each meeting versus the number that could have been used through two-sided reduction. Translate this into photocopying cost, and the point will be sharpened.

Notecards. Cut (or tear on a sharp table edge) normal-sized sheets of paper into quarters.

Scratchpads. Cut paper into your favorite pad size. Put even edges together. Clamp them in some way and smear the even edge with several coats of white glue. Let dry with the glue side up. If you have access to a paper-cutter, you can cut the sheets precisely and draw designs on the sides. *Or* cut the paper to fit a tin or small box and put it near the telephone.

(Decorate the box and make it a gift—with a year's supply of paper.) *Or* simply staple a bunch together. For recycled humor (or wisdom) use old one-a-day calendar slips.

Cards. Cut off the message and send the card again as a note or postcard. If you buy a card, add a note and keep the card intact. One card could have a long and cheering life!

Computer Paper. The ease with which we can "print out a rough draft" makes computers (which could lead to the saving of paper) a real paper-waster. So when you do print out a rough draft more than a few pages long, leave the perforations on and use the reverse side. Be sure to put a line through the back side so you can tell the second draft from the first!

File Folders. Federal express and paperboard mailers make sturdy, colorful file folders. And of course, relabeling gives any file folder an almost indefinite life.

Envelopes. Buy or make your own lick-stick address labels (*not* self-stick, which will make the envelope unrecyclable). You can buy sheets of lick-stick paper at a good stationery store (see "Make It," chapter four)—and reuse envelopes. With all the bulk mail most of us get, we should never have to buy envelopes again. Heavy-paper colored ads (such as those from *National Geographic*) can be folded into attractive envelopes.

Mailers. Most mailers can be opened carefully (at the stapled end) and used many times. Develop an obstinate pride at how many times you and your friends can send the mailers back and forth to each other.

Wrapping Paper. Colored ads that come in the mail (especially those with gorgeous wildlife or scenery pictures) can make beautiful small-package gift wrap. Comics make colorful gift wrap. Find the comic strip to fit your friend or the gift. Use odd pieces of string or yarn to make string-art ties.

Mulch. Put newspaper down and cover with straw for a good garden mulch. Paper is, after all, partially composted vegetable fiber.

Package Padding. Make your padding count: use local newspapers with items of interest, church bulletins, office memos. We've learned this from our daughter: every bit of her packaging and wrapping tells us something about what's up with her family.

Play Houses. The huge boxes from refrigerators and other large appliances make the best play houses. Cut doors and windows, and turn kids loose for home decor, renovation and rearrangement.

Warning: Take all this as a game of outwitting the garbage trap, but don't let every piece of wasted paper burden your conscience. If some of these suggestions seem tacky or trivial, pick ones that don't and try them—or find your own ways to escape the paper trap.

REUSE CONTAINERS

Packaging that we're stuck with—despite all efforts to reduce that half of our garbage—we can often convert to other uses. Like paper, containers are a major component of landfill. But unlike paper, a lot of containers are, at present, hard to recycle (especially in some areas). And recycling anything involves energy, so reuse is better.

We've listed here a few uses for the kinds of containers that come home with most of us on just about every shopping trip.

Egg Cartons. Many small stores and chicken farmers will gladly take these from you and reuse them. Just ask. Styrofoam egg cartons make excellent seedling starters (the cups) and drip trays (the tops). Nursery schools find endless uses for egg cartons.

Cardbord Frozen Concentrate Juice Containers. These are invaluable for soap and candle-making. See chapter four, "Make It."

Bleach or Oil Plastic Containers. Leave the handle on, but cut a good-sized hole on the opposite side, and use for your toilet brush. Kept clean and tucked away behind the toilet, it will look quite normal. Cut off the top (including the handle) and you have an excellent funnel. Cut off the bottom and you have an excellent drip-tray or planter. Cut the sides into triangular strips for seedling identification tags (the white plastic is easy to write on).

Glass Jars. With care you can reuse most of your glass jars. With help from a few jar-using friends, you'll never need to buy jam, jelly, or canning jars.

—Jars with a plastic ring inside the lid: As long as the lid is not warped and the plastic ring is in good condition, these will reseal again and again for canning jams, jellies, homemade juices, and highly acidic foods like tomatoes. (Don't reuse seals for more spoilable things like meat or beans.)

—Jars with "regular" or "wide-mouth" lids: If you have a choice, buy foods in jars that will fit these two standard sizes of homecanning lids—for two reasons. First, most of these are every bit as durable as store-bought canning jars and can be used for canning your own vegetables or fruit. Second, you'll build up a supply of jars with only two sizes of interchangable lids, which will save you a lot of hunting around. Here are some things your jars are good for:

1. Refrigerator storage: Since glass is transparent, you'll be able to see, identify, and thus not waste all those little bits and dabs (especially if you put all your leftovers in one section).
2. You'll have a great food storage system for all the bulk dried foods you bring home (in your reused plastic bags).
3. Nut and bolt storage: Nail the lid to a beam in your garage, shop, or storage area, and unscrew the jar when you want its readily visible contents.

Plastic Buckets. (Such as large ice-cream containers.) These are invaluable for cleaning, storage, and all sorts of round-the-house use.

Plastic Sour Cream and Yogurt Containers. Here you can save a lot of frustration if you systematically buy the same kinds; this saves you the bother of flipping *your* lid as you scramble to find the right lid. Identical containers also stack nicely. They are useful for freezing produce or leftovers. (Get a good indelible marker for identification.) Also use them for plant pots. Put a few holes in the bottom, and use the lid as a drip base.

Plastic Bags. We seem to collect endless hordes of these, no matter what we do. Here are some helps.

—Take care of them so they last. Don't close them with impossible knots; use twist-ties (which also seem to accumulate).
—Keep them clean. Make a plastic-bag "porcupine" to dry them. Cut or plane one side off a fairly heavy twelve to fifteen inch log (or any heavy piece of wood) so it will lie flat; drill holes at least one inch deep in the log, at many angles and levels. Cut doweling about two feet long and stick the pieces in the holes. Round off the tops so they don't tear the bags. Set in an out-of-the-way place. We can dry about twenty at a time.

—Put them in your car-packaging box. (See "Packaging" in chapter one.)

Paper and Plastic Shopping Bags. Many thrift stores and food co-ops will welcome your collection with open arms. It saves them a great deal of packaging overhead, and it's a lot of fun carrying home your Salvation Army purchase in a Saks Fifth Avenue bag!

An important reminder:
  Refuse first,
  Reuse if you can't refuse,
  Recycle what you can't reuse.

REUSE... JUST ABOUT EVERYTHING ELSE (*AND* THE KITCHEN SINK)

We often decide far too hastily that something is useless, and in throwing it away we further degrade creation. So here's the low-down on reusing your own (and other people's) junk.

Rags.
—Save for a ragbag of uses: oiling or finishing; cleaning the toilet; wiping up messes; washing windows.
—Send them to the Salvation Army (if you can bear to part with them). Many thrift stores welcome rags. And at least one environmental catalogue actually sells them. (But don't buy a bag of rags; collect your own.)
—Some rags are better than others:

  Cotton rags. For most uses, cotton works best, as we discover with chagrin when we try to wash a window with polyester or hold a hot pan with a slightly damp fiber-fill hot pad. When you buy something, think what kind of a rag it will make.

Old mattress pads, blankets, fleecy coat linings, prefold diapers, and old quilted bed spreads. These make great quilt liners, hot or cold insulators, and hot pads.

Diapers. Regular, nonfolded diapers that are still good make the *best* dish towels. They're even sold for that purpose.

Drippings. Keep a small coffee or nut can (the kind with a tight plastic lid) in the fridge and add to it drippings: bacon grease, chicken fat, any grease that will harden. When it's full, freeze it. Once a year—or every other year—make soap or candles. Five pounds (or ten cups) makes over forty bars of soap. (See soap recipe in chapter four.)

Vegetable Juices. Drain these off of canned or cooked vegetables. Keep a plastic ice cream bucket or a quart yogurt container in the freezer: add all the juices. When you have enough, make a big pot of soup with these succulent juices as your water. See *The Frugal Gourmet*, by Jeff Smith, for a lot more ideas about cooking with leftovers.

Bones. Chicken bones especially can have a future. After cutting off all the meat, freeze the bones. When you have a potful, cover with your leftover vegetable juices and make chicken soup with rice. Make pea soup with ham bones, beef vegetable soup....

"Old Favorite" Fabrics. Save all those old favorites—the dresses and shirts that the kids were wearing in the scrapbook pictures or that you wore to special events, the nicest part of the ratty-old loved-to-bits baby blanket, the tablecloth you all sat down to for ten years, the old curtains—and make a memory quilt.

Old Saucers. Use these for plant-pot bases.

Cans with Plastic Lids. Save for Christmas food gifts.

Magazines. Invaluable for school projects, reference, browse material, and cut-out scrapbook collections for sick children.

The Kitchen Sink. Remodeling often results in "garbage" of perfectly good sinks, tubs, flooring, and light fixtures. Put an ad in the paper, set the unwanted item out in the alley on "large item collection day," take it to a thrift shop, or save it. "Who knows when you'll need it? If you throw it away, you'll wish you hadn't someday." (But maybe you can find one in someone else's garbage.)

For lots more ideas on reuse, see *Heloise: Hints for a Healthy Planet* (New York: Putnam Perigee, 1990).

BUY REUSABLES

Don't choose what you can't reuse.
  —A British borough council campaign slogan

❧

In the Store. Reuse means *use*—lots of it, the more the better. So when we make any purchase, we need to ask ourselves:

—Is this going to last?
—Is it repairable? Better yet, can I repair it? (See Wendell Berry's criteria for a new tool in "Tools," chapter six.)

Before buying an appliance, call a general appliance repair shop. Be sure that it repairs appliances of the type you're buying and that it does not *sell* them. (Vested interests drastically reduce objectivity!) Someone there will generally be able to make helpful suggestions about quality.

The library can also provide helpful information. For cars the best help is *Lemon Aid* (to keep you from buying a "lemon"). This gives detailed data on the problems that have shown up in all models of all cars over the last several years. *Consumer Reports*, a monthly magazine, has regular articles covering most makes of cars and their good and bad points.

For appliances try *Consumer's Digest and Consumer Reports.* Be careful to read the article through or hunt up the monthly issue that covers the research in detail. Sometimes the factors that give an appliance a good or bad score may not even apply in your circumstances. For instance, electric starters on a gas stove are valuable for many reasons and save energy, but they are worthless in rural areas where the electricity can be off for several days at a time and you're buying a gas stove so you don't have to rely on electricity!

In general, from chicken pot pies to thermal blankets to eco-friendly ads, *Consumer Reports* might have a listing worth checking.

Out of the Store. Sometimes high-quality used things are available right in your neighborhood.

Demolition sales. Oak flooring and trim, toilets, tubs, wash basins, light fixtures, doors, and doorknobs are often available for very little—sometimes just for the effort of salvage and removal. This is the only good feature in our creation-wasteful practice of bulldozing old homes and trucking them off to a landfill.

Garage sales. Garage sales are often filled with brand new or very slightly used goods. We have a brother-in-law who frequents garage sales. Most Christmas presents from that family are beautiful brand new or slightly secondhand garage sale goodies.

Thrift stores. Support a helping organization (which usually provides employment opportunities for low-income or handicapped people). If you're looking for a hard-to-find high-quality item that is often hard to get (like an old-fashioned, wavy-edged bread knife that you can sharpen), discriminating monthly browsing in places such as St. Vincent de Paul, Salvation Army, and Mennonite thrift stores may turn it up. And once again, you're giving an old object new life. But be careful: bargain-hunting for its own sake can be addictive and wasteful.

The back alley. Many communities have large-item collection days on which furniture, appliances, and other items are put out in the alley or by the street to be picked up for destruction. Don't assume these items are worthless. Sometimes they are perfectly good and their owners just don't want to haul them away or organize a garage sale. (And you might even be able to replace the occasional missing arm or leg.)

Final Warnings. Say no to bargains and freebies you really don't need or have time to fix. Ask the same questions you should ask if you are buying something new. Although keeping something from the dump is a worthy goal, there's not much good accomplished in turning your own garage or basement into a storage space for items that you too will throw away untouched in a few months, years, or decades. Yes, we speak from experience and a full basement. Throwaway habits present the pack rat and dump scrounger with a cruel dilemma: did God create the earth to be turned into cheap goods and discarded? No. But did he create you and me to find a use for other people's trash? There the answer is not so clear.

Recycle

Generations come and generations go,
*   but the earth remains forever.*
The sun rises and the sun sets,
*   and hurries back to where it rises.*
The wind blows to the south
*   and turns to the north;*
round and round it goes,
*   ever returning on its course.*
All streams flow into the sea,
*   yet the sea is never full.*
To the place the streams come from,
*   there they return again.*
                —Ecclesiastes 1:4-7

ᴈᴇ

CREATION RECYCLES EVERYTHING, but human beings have always left garbage heaps. In some regions of the earth whole cities have been built on the garbage of previous cities—sometimes thousands of years of it. But in the late twentieth century, just as our throwaway tendencies are reaching their worst, we seem to be realizing that throwing things away is out of step with the rest of creation. Recycling is beginning to catch on.

Partly this change in attitude has resulted from a recognition of the foolishness and impossibility of our colossal wastefulness: North Americans throw away far more garbage than any other people—between three and four pounds a day for every person. Partly it has come from economic incentives: as resources and energy get more expensive, it's cheaper to recycle.

There are lots of reasons to be glad about this new willingness to recycle our waste: we'll fill our landfills more slowly; have less need to log or mine or drill for new raw material; do less damage to the air, to streams, to the water table. But Christians have a deeper reason to be glad about recycling. Everything we study in creation, from the stars and planets right down to plants and animals, is made from recycled materials. It's arrogant of us, whose task is stewardship of creation, to assume that we should make everything of new material, use it once, and throw it away forever.

The more we learn about creation, the more we are humbled by the fact that *nothing* of what God made is wasted. Consider this description of one atom in the original prairie ecosystem of what is now the American Midwest. It is taken from *Sand County Almanac*, by Aldo Leopold, which was published almost thirty years ago but still remains one of the best and most beautiful pictures of the intricate workings of ecosystems:

> X had marked time in the limestone ledge since the Paleozoic seas covered the land.... The break came when a bur-oak root nosed down a crack and began prying and sucking. In the flash of a century the rock decayed, and X was pulled out and up into the world of living things. He helped build a flower, which became an acorn, which fattened a deer, which fed an Indian, all in a single year.
>
> ... When the Indian took his leave of the prairie, X moldered briefly underground, only to embark on a second trip through the bloodstream of the land.

This time it was a rootlet of bluestem that sucked him up and lodged him in a leaf that rode the green billows of the prairie June, sharing the common task of hoarding sunlight. To this leaf also fell an uncommon task: flicking shadows across a plover's eggs. The ecstatic plover, hovering overhead, poured praises on something perfect: perhaps the eggs, perhaps the shadows, or perhaps the haze of pink phlox that lay on the prairie.

... When the first geese came out of the north and all the bluestems glowed wine-red, a forehanded deermouse cut the leaf in which X lay, and buried it in an underground nest... molds and fungi took the nest apart, and X lay in the soil again.... Next he entered a tuft of side-oats grama, a buffalo, a buffalo chip, and again the soil. Next a spiderwort, a rabbit, and an owl. Thence a tuft of sporobolus.[1]

And so on. The point of this essentially endless story is clear. In God's creation everything is recycled, nothing is wasted. So after reducing and reusing, recycling is a prime duty of the stewardship of creation.

SOME OBSERVATIONS ABOUT RECYCLING

A great deal has been learned and written about recycling in the past few years—certainly more than we can include here. Much of this recycling wisdom and experience is summed up in a little book called *The Recycler's Handbook: Simple Things You Can Do*, (Berkeley, California: EarthWorks Press, 1990). Most of what we cover here is covered in greater detail in that book and others like it.

Since recycling is spreading very rapidly, it's hard to make generalizations that are true everywhere. A growing number of communities have curb-side recycling, which makes the job much easier. Others have recycling depots. Some recycling centers take plastics; others don't—yet. And so on. You can't start recycling without talking to some other people in your community, which is another good thing. Recycling has a way of drawing communities together. So for Christians it's a good way (in God's words to Jeremiah) to "seek the peace and prosperity of the city" where you live.

Industries, schools, businesses, and farms have their own waste problems, and these problems are substantial. But the largest single source of recyclable waste is the individual home. All of us contribute to this waste directly—and can do something about it directly.

There are two ends to recycling: supplying the materials to be recycled and then using what's made out of that recycled material. It's not enough to just recycle at the one end; we have to get in the habit of choosing and using recycled materials instead of their unrecycled equivalents. Sometimes what's produced from recycled material is essentially identical. But often it is different in color, texture, weight, and so on. So some change of habits and standards may be required in order for there to be both supply and demand to drive the recycling circle.

Often it may cost more to recycle or to buy recycled products. But it's important not to make all decisions on financial grounds alone. Recycling is worth doing even if it doesn't make immediate financial sense. In the long run it *does* make sense.

HOUSE WASTES

Let's start with the kitchen: most regular house waste passes through this all-important room. Once again, details will vary depending on what kind of recycling facilities are available in your area. But here are some general principles.

Separate Your Garbage. You'll need at least three containers. Good solid cardboard boxes or wooden fruit boxes work well, preferably with handles in the ends. Resist the temptation to *buy* new containers to recycle in!

1. Glass, metal, and plastic. Since these materials will have to be sorted again before you take them to the recycler, you might want to have a box for each material, perhaps even separate boxes for different colors of glass. But if you're short on space, put everything in one box and sort it later as needed.

   Jars and cans should be washed. Labels may or may not need to be removed (they come off easily when washing), depending on the requirements of your recycling center. Cans should be smashed. When the ends are out they crush easily underfoot. Put the ends in the can before smashing. Kids and frustrated adults usually like the can-smashing job—a few minutes of noisy, wholly legitimate mayhem. Again, check with your local recycler: some community compacters don't work well with presmashed cans.

2. Compostible material: peelings, eggshells, vegetable scraps, coffee grounds, tea leaves, and so on. Avoid meat scraps and grease: they smell and attract bugs and mice. It's best to have a water-tight container with a tight lid. The gallon tubs that ice cream comes in are ideal containers if kept under the sink. Or choose a more attractive container; put it on your countertop to make the whole job more accessible. And keep it *clean*. Put some cloves or lemon slices in the bottom if it gets smelly. Empty your container often, to avoid odor, into your compost pile, which we'll describe later under "yard waste." If your living situation doesn't allow a compost pile, you may be able to find a friend or neighbor eager to receive your offerings. Some more particulars about composting come later in this chapter, under "Compost Yard Waste."

3. Genuine throwaway trash: meat scraps, bones, and kinds of paper, glass, and plastic that for some reason

can't be recycled. This category should dwindle to almost nothing.

4. If you have a fireplace or woodstove, you might want to keep some paper products in yet another container. They make moderately good kindling if not heavily coated or inked. Most paper, however, can be recycled and we'll discuss that under "Paper Waste."

The golden rule of recycling is "Follow the Instructions." If you think the recyclers might accept something more—for example, they ask for aluminum cans, but you want to give them lawn furniture—ask. Ask what they take and how they want it prepared; then follow their rules precisely. The eager beaver who adds one ceramic coffee cup to the glass bin may render a whole lot of glass unsalable.

—Hannah Holmes, "Recycling 101,"
Garbage, March/April, 1991, 39.

BUILDING MATERIALS

Ordinarily the kitchen is the biggest source of waste—apart from paper, which we'll deal with separately. There is, however, one infrequent but significant household activity that's a major cause of waste: remodeling and building.

Reuse Building Materials. Construction debris is second only to paper products in the volume of landfills. But if you're doing a remodeling project, you can, with a little time, reduce considerably the amount you throw away. Up to ninety percent of construction materials can be recycled.

The most obvious recyclable material from remodeling projects is wood. Unless it's rotted, a fifty-year-old two-by-four is likely to be *better* than a new one. It does take longer to build with old wood. It's more prone to split under handling, and you must always be on the alert for hidden nails. But the satisfaction of knowing you've given the wood from that long-dead tree a new role to play is worth the time.

Wood that is too short, or splintered, or nail-filled to be re-used should still not be thrown away: it makes good fuel for a fireplace or stove. And you don't have to buy or wreck saws to cut it: anything from two-by-fours on down can be easily *broken* with a sledge hammer, and bigger pieces can be split.

Windows, doors, and almost all hardware can be reused. And brass or copper plumbing and electrical fixtures have real dollar value to the recycler.

Give Others a Chance to Reuse Building Materials. If you can't use, burn, or otherwise recycle old building materials, put up a sign that they are available. You'll probably have some takers. (We speak out of hours of urban back-alley roaming in search of free firewood.) You'll have more success in getting rid of old building materials if you clean them up and put them in some order. It's more work than consigning them to the garbage; but it's a small way of caring for creation.

Avoid Material that Can't Be Reused or Safely Disposed of. Unfortunately, some materials—notably sheetrock wallboard—are utterly unrecyclable, and their leachate is so noxious that many dumps refuse them. About all you can do with such materials is try to find a substitute, so the person who remodels after you will be spared the problem.

The same goes for many excess paints, adhesives, solvents, and fixatives: there simply isn't a suitable way of disposing of them. The only responsible thing to do is keep them in their can, in your own hazardous waste storage. This presents a good argument for either avoiding their use or choosing very carefully the amount you buy. Many communities have a hazardous waste collection day, but that just passes the problem along.

COMPOST YARD WASTES

> *Now I am terrified at the Earth, it is that calm and patient,*
> *It grows such sweet things out of such corruptions,*
> *It turns harmless and stainless on its axis, with such endless*
>   *successions of diseas'd corpses,*
> *It distills such exquisite winds out of such infused fetor,*
> *It renews with such unwitting looks its prodigal, annual, sumptuous crops,*
> *It gives such divine materials to men, and accepts such leavings*
>   *from them at last.*
> —Walt Whitman, "This Compost"

Organic waste is in a class by itself when it comes to recycling. For although almost everything else you recycle has to be hauled away and processed, through composting you can turn vegetable scraps and yard waste into rich soil in your own backyard—or with a little more care, in your own apartment. Since yard and food waste make up over a quarter (by volume) of what we throw away (more than glass, plastic, and metals combined), composting makes a substantial reduction in garbage. Some communities, running short of space to dump, are already *requiring* composting of yard wastes.

But there are more positive reasons to compost your organic garbage. The most obvious one is that composting produces soil. The value of soil is plain to anyone who grows a garden, and we'll talk more about it when we get to gardening (in "Part III: Spring"). If we grow food for our table from that soil, we have successfully "closed the circle," deliberately re-entered the cycles in which creation moves.

But one preliminary caution as we get down to the realities of composting, which is a pretty earthy business. Don't be daunted by all of the materials, techniques, books, and testimonials about composting. They are all merely ways of speeding up a process that *will* happen if you give it a chance. Wastes put back in the ground *will* compost: we couldn't stop the process if we tried. The simplest way is to dig a hole in the ground and dump your wastes in, digging deep enough so animals can't dig the stuff out.

Many books and pamphlets describe faster or more satisfying methods. Here are the essentials:

What to Compost. Use your kitchen scraps, as described earlier in this chapter, and yard wastes: leaves, young weeds (old ones have seeds) and grass clippings (though most cut grass should be left to compost on your lawn). The process will be speeded up if you chop compostibles into smaller pieces, but this isn't necessary.

The Compost Pile. Layer the material in a pile at least three feet on a side. Preferably, build a bin of wood or wire to contain it. It's good to have the pile in a well-drained place, out of the sun (whose warmth may dry it out), with some possibility of being covered. The pile should heat up through decomposition. Turn the pile occasionally (every month or so in the summer), and keep it moist.

It's obviously easier to have a bin with at least two boxes: one to hold new material, one to sit composting quietly away. A good general resource is Stu Campbell, *Let It Rot: The Gardener's Guide to Composting* (Pownal, Vermont: Storey Communications, 1990).

Apartment Compost. You can make good compost in an apartment or on an apartment balcony or patio. Here a book by Mary Appelhoff, *Worms Eat My Garbage*, is a valuable resource. It is available from Flower Press (1982), 10332 Shaver Rd., Kalamazoo, MI 49002. For more on small-scale composting, see "Soil" in chapter seven.

PAPER WASTE

Paper is by far the largest single item in our garbage—about fifty percent by volume.

Fortunately, paper is relatively easy to recycle. We have recycled newspapers for a long time. But the need for recycling is becoming more urgent, driven by both ends of our one-way use chain. Not only are we running out of places to throw our paper, but we keep using up our forests in order to supply our paper needs.

Paper comes from trees. Americans buy over sixty million newspapers a day and throw out about forty-four million, more than two-thirds of them. We destroy up to half a million trees to make those discarded papers—every day. When the psalmist wrote that the trees of the field clap their hands, he didn't mean that they were rejoicing at the prospect of being made into newsprint. Trees grow, that's true, and they don't have to grow very big or be of very good quality before their fibers are usable in paper. There's nothing wrong with treating some of our forests as tree farms for the purpose of producing paper. But often the trees logged for newsprint are in poor soils or harsh climates and don't grow back well. Or else they are managed in stands that make poor substitutes for forests. So we have good reason to encourage the recycling of paper in general and newspaper in particular. Here are some things we can do.

Recycle Your Newspapers. Tie them in a manageable bundle and get them to the recycling center. Some communities pick up at the curb; others have drop-off points. Paper should be clean and shouldn't be mixed with magazines or other coated paper.

Most paper recyclers won't handle glossy paper, since it is coated with clay—up to a ton of clay for every ton of wood-fiber. This may change, however, so keep checking. And if possible, cut down on your use of glossy paper. Share more magazines, which are the biggest coated-paper users.

Recycle Cardboard. Keep cardboard boxes clean and dry. If there's no prospect of reusing them, flatten them and take them to your recycling center. These are very good material for recycling, because the wood fibers in them are long and strong and can be recycled many times. (The fibers in paper shorten and degrade with each processing, so they are usable no more than about seven times.)

Recycle Office Paper. Make sure that any office you work in or frequent is set up to recycle paper, and encourage others to recycle. Although we currently recycle much less office paper than newsprint, office paper is a good thing to recycle because most of it is already highly bleached. Unlike newsprint or "cardboard [Kraft] paper," there's no need to bleach it—and the paper-bleaching process is not kind either to water or to air. There ought to be a box at the door of our churches to collect bulletins every Sunday. Perhaps you can think of a way of cutting down on such use—through overhead projectors, or order-of-service booklets kept in the pew.

Check with your recycler for guidelines on separating types of office paper for recycling. White and mixed colors will be processed differently. Using soy-based inks in copying machines will greatly reduce the toxicity of the recycling process.

Recycle Phone Books. The "low end" of the paper chain, as far as recycling quality goes, includes phone books, printed on low-quality, short-fiber paper. Some phone companies are beginning to pick up phone books for recycling, or at least make them in such a way that they can be easily recycled. Here a little judicious pressure on your phone company (let your fingers do the walking!) might help. Phone books in America take 650,000 tons of paper a year.

Recycle "Mixed Paper." Egg cartons, toilet-paper rolls, envelopes, and junk mail are at the *lowest* end of the paper chain. Sometimes these are accepted by paper recycling companies for such uses as roofing paper. Since a surprising amount of the paper that passes through our homes is in this miscellaneous category, it's worth trying to find a way to reuse it.

Because of the relative ease and popularity of recycling, there is currently a glut of paper to recycle. Mills need to be set up to take recycled paper, and they have been slow to adapt to the new market. It is very important that we keep pressure on the mills both by continuing to prepare waste paper for recycling, and (more importantly) by demanding to use recycled paper. If consumers refuse to buy paper that isn't recycled, manufacturers will very quickly get the point. But the world of recycled paper is complicated.

GUIDELINES FOR BUYING RECYCLED PAPER

1. Use recycled paper whenever possible, and let people know it is recycled. This is especially true of church bulletins: people need to know *that* they're printed on recycled paper and *why*.
2. Ask for "post-consumer" recycled paper. Much paper sold or advertised as recycled is made up of wastes internal to the paper plant that have never actually been used. Insist that the paper be "post-consumer"; otherwise the paper-recycling network is not strengthened.
3. Avoid bleached paper. Much "virgin" and recycled paper is bleached to an unnecessary whiteness, and the dioxin effluent from the bleaching process is nasty and destructive. We need to get in the habit of using off-white paper—

usually a pleasant light tan or gray—rather than demanding pure white.

4. Use recycled paper for photocopying. Some recycled papers don't work as well in copy machines or printers. If you, your church, or your office is buying a machine that handles paper, make sure it will handle recycled paper.

5. Buy recycled paper products whenever you can at your local store.

If you have trouble finding recycled paper and stationery, here are two excellent mail order sources: "The Paper Source," Fallbrook, Ontario, Canada K0G 1A0; and Earth Care Papers, Inc., P.O. Box 7070, Madison, WI 53707-7070. The latter also publishes a regular information booklet and donates ten percent of its pretax profits to organizations working on finding solutions to social and environmental problems.

AUTO WASTES

In a century littered with earth-changing inventions, the car has had a more devastating impact on creation than any of the rest. Not that the automobile is an intrinsically bad thing, but the seductive ease it gives us has fostered creation-ignoring and creation-destroying attitudes. Many of us feel that we depend so absolutely on the car that we could not possibly give it up. But much of that dependence is a delusion: walking, biking, sharing rides, and using public transportation could vastly reduce the number of miles we drive and the number of vehicles we "have to" own.

In later chapters we'll talk about some of the things we can do to begin to change our car-dependent attitudes. But here we're concerned with one specific way in which we can reduce the damage cars do to creation: that is, by recycling automotive waste products.

Of course, the first and most serious waste product from the car cannot be recycled: that's the byproducts from burning gasoline. One gallon of gas combines with oxygen to produce about twenty-two pounds (much more than a gallon weighs!) of carbon dioxide. It's no surprise that the percentage of carbon dioxide in the atmosphere has increased steadily in the last few decades. There's absolutely no way that this combusted fuel can be recovered, reused, or recycled. The only ways to stop that waste are to drive less, have more efficient engines, and use different fuels.

But there are other waste products from cars that can and should be recycled.

Motor Oil. Lots of people change their own oil, which is a good thing to do. However, used motor oil is a particularly noxious substance. The oil from a single oil change can ruin a million gallons of water. Unfortunately, of the 200 million gallons of used oil drained by Americans from their cars every year, about 120 million gallons are simply thrown away: poured down sewers, put in trash cans, or dumped on the ground. That's more than ten times the amount lost in the Exxon Valdez spill. About sixty-two percent of oil-related pollution in the United States is from used motor oil. This doesn't count the amount handled by garages. Most but not all of that oil is now recycled. Make sure that the garage you use recycles its oil.

Recycling oil is simple—for you. Collect it in a container with a good lid, and take it to an oil recycling center or to a garage that will accept it. Make sure no other toxic materials (paint, pesticides) are mixed with the oil. Only about sixty percent of old oil is recovered, but that's enough to save every day over half the output of the Alaska pipeline and more than one-eighth of U.S. daily consumption.

Recycled oil is as good as new and can be recycled indefinitely. It's important that there be markets for it; so when you have a chance, buy recycled oil.

Tires. In North America we use up and throw away about one tire per person per year. Most of these end up in landfills or huge tire piles, which often catch fire and release large amounts of pollution.

Tires aren't easy to recycle, but we're learning. Whole tires can be fastened together as reefs or erosion stoppers. Ground up, they've been used in brake linings and as an additive to asphalt paving. An attractive new use that is doubly kind to creation is in the manufacture of "soaker hoses." These hoses leak intentionally, through pores in the rubber, to add slow, water-saving moisture to your garden.

The best way to keep from adding tires to the waste stream is by driving less and by making sure that your tires are properly inflated and aligned. But eventually you'll have to discard your tires, and then it's important to know that some tire manufacturers and dealers do recycle. Seek them out. And retreaded tires are a good way of getting more life out of the rubber, so buy them when you can.

Air-Conditioning Fluid. Till recently, the freon and other CFC's (chlorinated fluorocarbons) in car and home air conditioners were not a source of worry. They leaked out, evaporated, and were gone. But now we know they're not gone: they go into the upper atmosphere where they devour ozone. The chemistry of what happens is complex, but each CFC molecule is capable of destroying up to one hundred thousand molecules of ozone. The layer of ozone that shelters the earth from ultraviolet radiation is one of the Creator's recently discovered gifts. But it appears that this layer is thinning rapidly, and a major culprit is the activity of these gasses. Solvents, aerosols, foam insulation—and air conditioners—are the major sources.

There is a major attempt internationally to reduce CFC pollution, in part by the development of suitable substitutes. But one of the strategies is the use of coolant-sucking machines (nicknamed "vampires") in service stations. These remove the coolant from the system and store it for recycling. If you have a car air conditioner, make sure it is serviced by someone who has a machine like this to retrieve and store the coolant.

Batteries. Batteries hold about 18 pounds of lead and a gallon of sulphuric acid. About one-fifth of car batteries get discarded, adding about 330 million pounds of lead and almost fifty million gallons of sulphuric acid to landfills. Your gas station will take your battery for recycling.

Car Frames and Bodies. In North America every year we throw away enough iron and steel to supply our entire car industry. The majority of this is in car bodies and engines. When you're through with a car—really through with it—make sure that it doesn't sit and rust somewhere but gets recycled through a junk yard.

There are other ways to recycle cars. Some regions have incorporated old car bodies in erosion-stopping dikes. And on the island where we live, most engine blocks end up in some cove or bay as an ideal anchor for a buoy, often made out of a foam-filled old tire!

PART TWO

WINTER

THINGS TO DO

❄ Savor and share the beauty of creation by making things which "selve" the distinctness of individual creatures.
❄ Make gifts that involve the whole family.
❄ Enjoy the intricate variations of shape and texture in everyday basics such as wood and food.
❄ Decorate your home with God's art from the natural world.
❄ At Christmas decorate your tree and your home with things that bring together natural beauty, family creativity, and a focus on the birth of Jesus.
❄ Next year, try a no-buy, make-it-yourself Christmas.
❄ Make the day after Christmas a celebration of creation— the goodness of both the natural world and each other.
❄ Keep things in good repair.
❄ Keep "fix-it" skills alive by using the services of repair people.
❄ Consider guidelines for longtime (even lifetime) use when purchasing new tools.
❄ Develop your own "fix-it" skills and share those skills with others.
❄ Learn how things work.
❄ Distinguish carefully between "needs" and "wants."
❄ WAIT and MAKE DO as a way to kick the buying habit.
❄ Don't use this book as an excuse to buy a whole new set of gadgets.
❄ Develop hobbies which DON'T involve you in a lot of "getting" and DO involve you with the variety of creation.
❄ Form a community tool-sharing agreement with neighbors or friends for large, expensive, and infrequently-used tools.
❄ Turn your church kitchen into a canning and/or jam and jelly making center for a day.

❋ Hunt for vacant lots or right-of-ways in cities that can be made into community garden plots.

❋ Look for people in your church or neighborhood who can share knowledge or skills involving the world of creation.

❋ Experience "A Meal at the World's Dinner Table" with your church or Bible study.

❋ Give up a meal and donate the cost to world relief.

❋ Treat a street person to a good and nourishing meal.

❋ Invite some newcomers to church home with you for coffee or a meal.

❋ Spend time with your friends over a potluck breakfast.

❋ Make meals a time for celebrating the rich gifts of God in the bounty of his creation.

❋ Read good books to each other!

MEDITATION

Christmas and Creation

... the Word within
The world and for the world;
and the light shown in darkness and
Against the Word the unstilled world still whirled
About the centre of the silent Word.
                        —T.S. Eliot, "Ash Wednesday"

Joy to the world! the Lord is come:
Let earth receive her king,
Let every heart prepare him room,
And heaven and nature sing.
                        —Christmas Carol

CHRISTMAS IS THE REMEMBRANCE OF THE INCARNATION; that astonishing and mysterious gift by which the Creator entered his creation. That event which we celebrate (and all too often trivialize) is in itself a powerful reason for us to care for creation. For if at creation God said, "It is good," in the Incarnation God says in effect, "It is *very* good." *Incarnation* means "enfleshment," but the more we know about our "flesh," the more we realize all that God took upon himself.

God the Creator became not only man: he became animal; he became organism. (For though we are more than animal, we *are* animal—and share DNA with the lowliest organism.) He entered into those processes of inhaling and exhaling, eating and excreting, living and dying, that make the circle such an apt symbol for creation. In doing so he hallowed them. Or rather, he reacknowledged and revealed their hidden holiness. As Athanasius wrote, "no part of creation had ever been without Him Who, while ever abiding in union with the Father, yet fills all things that are."[1] In the Incarnation God began to share with creation in a new way, and to show us what we all dimly know: that creation is a gift, the original and greatest gift.

It is appropriate then that Christmas be a time of celebrating God's gifts: the original gift of creation and the restoring gift of his Son.

History gives no clue as to the actual time of year in which the birth of Jesus took place. But very early it came to be associated with a pagan festival celebrating the winter solstice. This was no trivial event in the circle of the year. We who can obtain light and warmth at the touch of a finger on a switch can hardly understand the length, the dark, the cold of winter nights throughout most of human history. Hunger, sickness, and death were far more common in that dark time of the year.

So the gradual return of the sun is not a piece of astronomical trivia: it is like the gift of life itself. It is symbolically right that we remember God's gift of Jesus at this dark time of the year.

Christmas is a celebration of God's gift of creation and of creation renewed. So in our care of creation, the yearly celebration of Christmas can remind us of several year-round principles.

Certainly one of them is that we ought to take more seriously the gifts of light and warmth. The candle and the hearth are ancient and accurate symbols of the gift of "the Father of lights." So there *is* a celebratory place for a blazing hearth and a glory of lights. But our very delight in these things should help us remember the points about energy made in the last chapter. For though the energy that lights and warms our homes is the Creator's gift, we often squander it at a high price to creation.

We need to pause here to apologize to readers in the southern hemisphere and the tropics, for whom the whole framework of this book—and especially the symbolism of returning light at Christmas—does not exactly apply. Australians, New Zealanders, and other antipodeans are long used to the irony of Christmases being associated with cold, snow, and coziness, when the outdoor reality suggests instead a picnic at the beach.

This seasonal difficulty reinforces a central fact of Christmas; it has been called the "scandal of particularity." Though God's gifts are to all creation, the birth of Jesus was at a particular place and time, not only in the cycles of the seasons but on the circle of the turning earth. To celebrate the birthday of Jesus on one date, all over the planet, is a reminder of that particularity. It would diminish its reality to make Christmas back into a festival celebrating the return of the sun, hence varying from place to place. Christians in the southern hemisphere can still appreciate the point about the returning of the light—even if it is necessary to *remember* what things were like six months earlier.

Another dimension of this dark time of the year is worth recalling, and it too is an appropriate part of the folklore of Christmas: it is the meaning of "home." Theologically, eschatologically, cosmically, the Incarnation makes us at *home* in creation. G.K. Chesterton caught the audacity of the divine gift when he wrote in "The House of Christmas":

To an open house in the evening
Home shall men come....
To the place where God was homeless
And all men are at home.[2]

Much of the richness of Christmas in our culture is its association with home. (Though recently that richness has become bittersweet as more homes break up or become less homelike.) This focus on homeyness is a good way of recalling not only that home is where many of the gifts of creation are used, it is also a reminder that home is where those gifts can be made or repaired into things humanly useful. We are reminded of the force of the idea of "home" through the word "homemade." None of us really believe it when the pies in the restaurant are advertised as "homemade," but the phrase makes us order a piece anyway. For lingering somewhere in all of us is the image of home as a place where food is prepared, tools are used and repaired, and life is centered on our relationship to creation. In the last few generations vast numbers of skills—from making soap to making cloth to making cheese—have been forgotten by all but a few professionals. The advantages of shifting these things out of the home and into the paid, public, and professional world are obvious: more time, more money, less bother, less drudgery.

The losses are perhaps less obvious, but they are profound. One is that making and repairing things at home kept the links between us and the created world much shorter and more obvious. Today, when all the processing from raw material to finished product is done somewhere else, by someone we will never see, and when the finished product is bought by us in a store from a rack containing dozens of identical things, it's easy for us to forget that we are creatures depending on creation. And more directly: though there are "economies of scale" associated with mass-production, there is also increased wastage, more use and disposal of toxic materials, more of creation wasted in order to package, market, transport, and preserve items for our convenience.

So though we do not want to suggest the undoing of our industrial economy, we think that in all sorts of real and symbolic ways we would be better off, better stewards of creation, if we did more at home. And Christmas is a good time to think about such regained skills, not only because of the midwinter impetus to be at home, but because Christmas giving is a chance to learn and perfect skills for the sake of the joy they will bring someone else.

Which brings us to a final lesson about caring for creation. Christmas began with the greatest gift of all, and it is remembered (even among many who ignore its origin) by gift-giving. Though we need to detach ourselves from the frenzy of consumption that climaxes just before Christmas, primarily gift-giving is sharing. It is a recognition that our very lives are nourished by exchange. Air, water, light, and food are creation's gifts to us, and Christmas is a time to remember how much we depend on the bounty of others. It is a time to relearn old lessons about sharing and about the care of creation that results from our life together.

❄ FOUR ❄

Make It

*And if the time come when machines have been so perfected as
to need no human guidance or supervision, or at most only a few
hours by a few men per day, even so Industrialism would still
mean that necessary things, houses, furniture, clothes and food,
things which during all the centuries of man's history have been
his chief means for pleasing himself, his only means of collaborat-
ing with God in creating, would be deprived of that beauty which
is the special mark of human work, the beauty of tenderness and
sensibility in the actual handling of material things.*
—Erik C. Gill, *A Holy Tradition of Working*

ONE OF THE CLAIMS MADE FOR industrial civilization is that
through the efficiency and speed of mass-production
we have been delivered from the drudgery of much of the
work that keeps a household going. True as that claim is, we
have to recognize another truth: much of the decline in the
health and integrity of creation dates from that same acceleration in labor-saving technology.

Furthermore, suicide rates are higher than ever, boredom, meaninglessness, and anomie are increasingly common modern complaints; and people spend more and more
to keep themselves amused and entertained. These things
suggest that ease has brought not happiness but restlessness.

Sixteen hundred years ago, in the twilight of another tired civilization, St. Augustine prayed, "O Lord, thou hast made us for thyself: and our hearts are restless till they find their rest in thee" (*Confessions*).

Sadly, many of us who say that through Christ we have found rest in the Creator are troubled by the same frantic restlessness as our secular contemporaries. Part of the problem is that though we have found a kind of rest in God, we have so distanced ourselves from his gifts in creation that we know little real joy.

Some of that joy is available through simply opening our senses. But another way of experiencing God's goodness in creation is through participating more fully and thoughtfully in the use we make of it. We need to work deliberately and thoughtfully at involving ourselves in at least some of the processes by which we turn creation's bounty to our own use. We need to learn again how to *make* things.

MAKE IT YOURSELF

What we make, whether for ourselves or for others, becomes far more than just a project or a product. We can see, touch, and maybe even hear a mobile of driftwood and beach glass; but only in the making do we learn about the bits of beauty—even in garbage—to be found in beach debris. In the end we'll love the beach, the birds, the ebb and flow of tides, the free salt air, more than we did before.

Here are some suggestions for making things yourself:

Start Simple. Make-it-yourself projects can consume too much time and money. Start with things that can be made with what you have and go on from there.

Start Young. Include the kids. Making things rather than buying them is a good habit to learn early—by watching and by helping.

Savor Creation. When we make things ourselves, we not only are likely to use materials that can be found close to home (thus avoiding some of the environmental costs of transport and manufacture), but we will better understand, appreciate, and savor those created things we use for our making. In both cases we are prepared to care better for creation.

"Selve" Creation. The great Christian poet Gerard Manley Hopkins spoke of the "inscape" of each created thing. He meant by the word those qualities that make a thing distinctly itself. He felt that through *our* words and actions, we ought to let the "inscapes" or "selves" of things speak with *their* own voice, shine with their own light.

MAKE-IT-YOURSELF GIFTS

Napkins, Napkin Rings, and a Napkin Ring Holder: These make good presents and are easy to make. Your friend may have lots of napkins; in that case make the rings and holder. The rings help keep straight whose napkin is which, and the holder solves what to do with the napkins between meals. Most important: all three enable us to stop the bad habit of using something once and throwing it "away." This backs up with action our mealtime words of thankfulness to God for his gifts of creation.

Napkins. Make them at least fifteen inch square, out of print material. The turned edge can be sewn by hand or machine. Napkins don't have to match. Variations on a color theme, or even wildly different patterns matched to the peculiarities of your friends, make it easier to keep napkins straight—and thus ensure reuse.

Rings. Make of wood at least one inch thick. A hardwood that won't split easily, like oak or walnut, is best. Mark the shapes you want on the board, and make holes (between 1 and 1-1/4 inch) in the middle of each shape. It's important to have different shapes, for ease of identification. Simple geometric shapes—squares, diamonds, triangles—can be cut quite easily on any table saw. Drill the holes, then cut the shapes. Sand lightly and oil. (Salad oil will do fine.)

Another possibility: Find a well-cured limb, slice it in one inch sections, and drill a hole through the center of each. (Here the only problem is figuring out a way to hold the slice while you're drilling.)

An attractive and wood-less alternative is to save "eye" bones of round steaks. Cleaned, dried, and polished they make attractive rings. Or cut a piece of heavy cardboard tubing into sections and cover them with fabric.

Holder: Hang something in your dining room to hang the napkins on. A piece of wood with pegs (cut from a section of dowel) inserted at an upward angle works fine. Or stick curtain hooks into a piece of wood. Use your ingenuity.

Grocery Bag. Make a reusable shopping bag with good heavy cloth. Be sure to reinforce the bottom with a double layer of cloth or a piece of vinyl. Handles should be easy to hold. For strength, extend the handles all the way down the sides and around the bottom.

Apron. Buy an inexpensive baker's or butcher's plain white cotton apron at a drugstore or a restaurant supply store. Decorate with fabric crayons. Iron to make decoration permanent. A personalized handmade apron makes men or women more likely to put it on and start making things from scratch.

Stationery. Press flowers, leaves, and grasses in the pages of an old telephone book. Your plant material will work best if it's not thick or fleshy. Weigh down the phone book with other books; wait a week. Then use thinned white glue (the sort that dries clear) to fasten single flowers or a collage on the front of a plain card.

Or use potatoes or sponges as printing blocks: dip them in watercolor or ink and "print" your cards. Or paste on copies of a favorite photo (it's often cheaper to make lots of copies at once). Or have the kids draw pictures with black pens: take the best of the lot and adjust the size with a photocopy machine to fit one side of a folded half sheet of paper.

Granola. Concoct your own combination of grains, nuts, and dried fruits. Give it away in reused tins or jars with your own labels. This idea can be adapted for candy, muffin mix, spice mixes, potpourri, and so on.

MAKE IT FROM SCRATCH

Food does not exist merely for the sake of its nutritional value.... A man's daily meal ought to be an exultation over the smack of desirability which lies at the roots of creation. To break real bread is to break the loveless hold of hell upon the world, and by just that much, to set the secular free.
—Robert Farrar Capon, *The Supper of the Lamb*

"From scratch" is an old expression of uncertain origin that means "make it yourself from whatever you have on hand." Perhaps it comes from having to "scratch around" in drawers, cupboards, and cellars to find ingredients. So making things "from scratch" is one way of "making do" (which we'll discuss shortly).

Here are some good reasons to make things from scratch:

—What we make is *really* homemade.
—We can choose, with our own discriminating taste, fresh, maybe even homegrown, ingredients.
—We can avoid transportation, energy use, toxic ingredients, excessive packaging—and save money.

—We can preserve and relearn forgotten skills for making careful use of creation.

—Few activities give us such a sense of accomplishment and deep-down satisfaction as getting our hands into the stuff of creation and making something from it.

One caution: Remember that most good things in life— like marriage—take patience, perseverance, and the ability to learn from mistakes. So making basic things from scratch can help us learn large lessons in small, character-forming doses. Don't give up if these things don't turn out perfectly the first or even the second time. (The best way to learn is to do it with a friend or relative who knows how.)

So from mayonnaise to marshmallows, many things that we assume must be bought at the store can be made easily and cheaply at home. By doing so we remove one more barrier between us and the created world.

We could at this point fill the book with recipes, but there are many books that do that for us so we've only included a starter—a good easy soap recipe. For food, one of the best is still *The Joy of Cooking*. (Yes, it has recipes for both mayonnaise and marshmallows.) Another useful book is *Back to Basics: How to Learn and Enjoy Traditional American Skills*, (Pleasantville, NY: The Reader's Digest Association, Inc., 1981) which describes with excellent detail and illustrations all sorts of once-common knowledge: preserving fruit; drying flowers; tanning leather; making cheese, soap, and candles.

Soap. This is *good* soap, not just some quaint curiosity, so making it can reduce your expenses. (See the section for tips on saving "drippings" in chapter two.) Two warnings:

1. This is *not* a good thing to do with children, because of the hot fat and lye.
2. Use stainless steel or glass containers—no aluminum.

3 cups clean fat—cooled but still pourable.
To clean fat: put drippings in a pan with an equal amount

of water. Bring just to a boil. Let it chill. Remove fat slab. If it doesn't look entirely clean, repeat. You can buy beef, pork, or lamb fat from the butcher, cut it into cubes and boil with water to extract the fat, then refine as above. Bacon drippings alone make fine soap, so does the usual household hodge-podge of meat grease. You can also substitute a hard, cheap margarine

1 cup cold water

5 tablespoons lye
Mix water and lye and let stand till cool.

Pour lye-water very slowly into fat, mixing continually (mix in a beater of blender, or use a stainless-steel wire whip). Continue mixing until mixture becomes slightly thickened.

3 tablespoons glycerine; scent (perfume or essential oil) *and color* (food coloring works fine—or stir in steamed red beet chunks for a beautiful pale rose color). Color will lighten as soap hardens.

Pour into molds (such as cardboard juice containers, or cut-off bottoms of milk cartons) and let harden (24–48 hours). Cut into sections. Let dry on a rack for a week. Wrap in waxed paper and use after storing for a least one month. Home-made scented soap bars make good presents. Flaked, (grated) it will clean your laundry!

Your Daily Bread. Bread is so important that we use the word almost as a synonym for food. Eating bread in all its various forms is one of the main ways we are sustained by creation. Jesus taught us to pray, "Give us this day our daily bread." And we accept God's gift of bread gladly, even from the supermarket. But we'd probably have a deeper appreciation for our bread if we made it ourselves: in all of creation there's hardly any smell or taste so simply *good* as that of freshly baked bread.

We often bake bread on Sunday evenings and thus end the Sabbath with fresh bread and butter. We make six loaves at once: that's the most you can fit in a normal household oven, and it supplies a hungry family of four for a week. After you've made bread a few times you'll be able to make it with only about twenty minutes of actual time invested. But the process can take four hours or more from start to finish, and the first time or two you'll be occupied for most of that time: checking, patting, poking, and vacillating between agony at potential failure and ecstasy that the yeast is actually doing its reliable work.

The only pieces of essential equipment for making bread are a large stainless steel or ceramic bowl (twelve or fourteen quart size) and six breadloaf pans. Try to to keep your bread pans just for baking bread. If the pans are new, oil them generously the first few times, up to and including the top edges. Don't wash them out after baking; after a while you'll get a good, reliable, non-stick surface.

MAKE IT BEAUTIFUL

We have been writing about caring for creation—but "care for" can mean two rather different things. It can refer to tending a sick patient, or it can mean *loving* someone or something for its own sake. The first kind of care doesn't necessarily involve the second: a person may nurse back to health someone he detests; he may give professional lawn (or car or carpet) "care" out of nothing more than commercial motives. So we don't necessarily love or delight in what we merely "take care of."

But the second kind of care always calls forth the first: what we love we will not only cherish, we will take care of.

It's easy for us, in this frantically practical age, to adopt the attitude of impersonal nurse toward the ailing earth. It's far better if our caretaking is rooted in the other kind of care: in love and delight.

Unfortunately, we have assumed that such care is the work

of a special kind of individual (the artist), to be put in a special kind of place (the museum or the gallery). So we buy mass-produced furniture, dishes, and clothes, and we assume that things made with love and care are too rare for our enjoyment or use.

Beauty is an elusive word. But much of what we call *"beautiful"* is the endless bounty and variety of creation made accessible to us through a human act or artifact. And all of us should thus be midwives to the beauty of creation. Indeed, Paul tells us, creation seems to be groaning in the pains of childbirth, waiting for midwives, husbandmen, to give it birth into beauty (Rom 8:18-25). An unfortunate modern distinction between "art" and "craft" has robbed us of much of the joy of God's creation. Here are some suggestions for restoring the beauty of creation to ordinary things we do and make.

Let Wood Be Wood. Most of our houses have wood in them in door frame, trim, molding, or furniture. Even the plainest of woods is a thing of beauty, shining through the curves and swirls of its grain a signature of the seasons of growth and quiet which the tree lived through before it was cut for our use. Thus it is a kind of denial of creation to paint bare wood in a way that obscures and neutralizes its *woodiness.*

Fine work with wood takes considerable skill, though it is a skill that anyone can learn. But everyone can do something with wood, whether it's cutting blocks for a child, stacking boards on bricks to make a bookcase, or installing paneling and trim. And it's a good idea to finish the wood with oil or stain. To do so is an act of caring, of stewardship. It assures that the wood's unique record of its own life is not covered up.

Many who live in old houses have discovered with delight—after considerable labor—that under layers of paint lies warm-grained wood. There are trade-offs here: some paint removers are toxic and dangerous chemicals. Select a method that minimizes the use of those chemicals, avoids contact or fumes, and disposes of toxins with care.

Let Food Remind You of Its Origin. We are so removed from the origins of our food that we are sometimes startled when it looks like what it is: fish or leaf or stem. It's easy for us to forget food's origin, which is in some other *created thing.* We are not suggesting that it is wrong to eat fellow creatures, but we ought to do so in a solemn awareness that we are sustained by life and beauty which we destroy. At least some of our food should be prepared and served in ways that make us aware of the beauty of what we're devouring. Don't chop the lettuce into green confetti: leave it in the curved, veined beauty of its form. Serve fish whole, not in sanitized chunks, to honor its form. Serve fruit and nuts so that people can appreciate the shapes and textures that hold their nourishment.

Decorate with God's Art. Our houses and apartments are spaces carefully designed to separate us from the unpleasantness of creation—rain, wind, cold, heat. Our windows look out onto the created world, and we bring creatures of earth, air, and water inside to sustain us. But there are other ways we can open the wall between ourselves and creation: simply by bringing created things into the house as emblems, symbols, reminders of that larger world. Stones from the beach can serve as bookends; a piece of driftwood on the mantle can be more interesting in its curves and textures than any sculpture. These decorations can remind us of the processes of fire, ice, wind, and water that formed them.

MAKE IT WITH OTHERS (ESPECIALLY AT CHRISTMAS)

"So Barbara Ann and Arlene cleared off the dinner and worked at it in the kitchen, worked at the wreckage, Barbara Ann just as glad nobody else had offered to help. Been a long time since she'd been alone with her mother in the kitchen, the kitchen where they'd spent so many hours together over the years. Working together, you know, with your hands busy, in the kitchen, you can say a lot of

things that you might not be able to say to each other at the table. If you said it at the table it would be too blunt, too dramatic, everybody would stare at you.

But you can work around in the kitchen, kind of a close silence there around you, working at things, and, without looking at someone, just... release these little sentences out into the air... "

— Garrison Keillor, transcript from
"Prairie Home Companion" broadcast

Garrison Keillor, that storyteller of small-town America, captures an important truth about human relationships. When our hands are busy and the focus is on this or that rather than on me or you, we are somehow more real for each other. Just as we can see an object more clearly in twilight if we focus off to one side of it, so while working with each other we can somehow sense each other's inner shape. Such goods as caring for creation, doing justice, and making peace will mean very little in the long run if we don't care for each other. And we cannot truly care for each other unless we know each other's hopes, fears, joys, and sorrows.

Christmas comes "in the bleak midwinter," when in ancient cultures families and friends would gather close to the fire and tell stories, sing songs, or play games. Through technology we have conquered the dark of midwinter. But often still the lengthening dark of those long cold days reaches deep into our hearts and souls. So we rush about in a week-long shopping spree, driving from one mall to another, spending money in one store after another, losing our tempers in one deep frustration after another with stores, malls, and (tragically) with each other. Then after Christmas come the bills.

Christmas is a celebration of Emmanuel, God with us; the Creator's ultimate gift to creation. But we often turn it into an anti-creational festival: denying God's creation in a frenzy of consuming it; denying each other in our frustrated attempts to please each other with gifts; denying the Incarnation of the Word through our very attempts to celebrate it.

It is right to celebrate Christmas by honoring the gift by which creation is being restored. One of the main ways to honor the God who has chosen to be *with* us is to make this a time of being *with*: with God, with our friends and family, with the creation God made. Here are some suggestions for making and keeping Christmas together.

The Tree. It's not a bad idea to buy a live tree and plant it once the season is over—provided the tree is suitable for your place and climate. But don't disdain cutting a tree for this one-time Christmas use. It is indeed a kind of sacrifice, but there is a place for sacrifice.

In every meal we draw on sacrificed life to feed our body, and there's no reason why once a season we shouldn't sacrifice a tree to feed our spirit. Its resinous incense should remind us, every time we enter the house, of the Bethlehem baby who grew up to be nailed to a tree, a sacrifice for us. The Christmas tree is related backward in time to Eden's tree of life, and forward to the cross. In our house we like to leave the Christmas tree up scandalously long, then burn it in a kind of Lenten ceremony, lopping the limbs off one by one till the dead tree's resemblance to the cross is unmistakable.

Decorating the Tree.

String popcorn and cranberries with needle and thread. Tie the sections together and loop them over the branches, munching the popcorn while you're at it. And when the season is over, drape the chain outside and let the birds recycle it.

Make gingerbread people. Decorate them to look like friends or relatives. With toothpicks for "brushes" and saucers of colored icing, you can go into as much detail as you have patience for. (Our friend Ruth once stayed up all night; and when we got up there we all were iced on cookies, complete to our hairdos and plaid shirts.)

Decorate with cookies. Use all sorts of cookie cutter shapes with a basic sugar-cookie dough and have a cookie-decorating party. Let these be your tree decorations. Put a quarter-inch hole in each cookie before baking if you want to hang them up.

Christmas-tree lights use electricity but they shouldn't necessarily be given up. Christmas-tree lights use electricity, and seem frivolous. Yet they cheer the spirits and shouldn't necessarily be given up. We use such enormous amounts of electricity for our own comfort that we can probably spare a little for celebrating the coming of the Light of the World. Here's a bargain you can make with yourself: only buy a string of Christmas lights when you've established that you've clearly saved that much energy regularly by a permanent change of habit. Then you'll be celebrating the Incarnation of the Word, "in whom all things hold together," in a double sense: with the lights and with a year-round care for creation.

Consider investing in a few Christmas-tree candles and holders. On Christmas Eve turn off all the lights, and light the candles, one by one. As the candles are lit, the room will get brighter and brighter, till the tree is aglow with flickering light and shadow. The bright tree is a beautiful image of the light God has given us in his Son—the light for each of us and for the whole room. Leave them lighted long enough to sing some carols, then extinguish them one by one and watch the growing forest of shadows on the ceiling! Leave enough candle so you can have at least one more candle-lit holy-day time before dismantling the tree.

Keep a close watch, of course, and keep water or a fire extinguisher close at hand. But in years of doing this we've never had an accident. The created architecture of evergreen trees—longer branches below, shorter ones above, slightly offset—keeps this from being as dangerous as it sounds.

The House.

Advent wreath. In late fall begins the season of Advent, a penitential preparation for the celebration of the Incarnation. The Advent wreath with its four candles suggests a cross imposed on a circle. Thus it hints at the event that gives meaning to creation—the entrance of the Creator into the cycles of nature, beginning with the birth in a stable and ending on the cross.

Make an Advent wreath to reflect on that event that gives meaning to "the ever-circling years." Cover a circular base of wood or styrofoam with evergreens to represent our never-changing God. Space four candles (traditionally a penitential red or purple) in holes around the ring. Place a pure white candle in the center. Light one additional candle on each of the four Sundays before Christmas, and the Christ candle on Christmas day.

Deck the halls—with boughs of holly if you can. It grows almost wild in our part of the world. But use at least some evergreen branches. One candle, lit at dusk in a window, hall, or bathroom, is a good reminder of the coming of the Light.

A crèche. The crèche dates from St. Francis of Assisi, who one Christmas Eve brought animals into the churchyard and said to the people, "Behold your God, a poor and helpless child, the ox and ass beside him. Your God is of your flesh."

A variation on the crèche, good with small children, is to place the animals and people throughout the house. The ones that would be at the stable first (like the cows) put close by; put the wise men in the farthest corner, and so forth. Move the pieces closer day by day, till on Christmas Eve the whole cast is there. Or save the wise men for the day after Christmas; it helps make the point that Christmas is not just one day!

Gifts. For one year, try a No-Buy Christmas.

Rule 1: Each present has to be made by hand, from materials in or within walking distance of the maker's home.

Rule 2: Presents must not be made off in a corner but out in the open. You can even ask the recipient to help. But never tell the recipient what you're making or whom you're making it for!

Just to get your mind ticking, here are a few ideas:

—Stuffed animals using fabric remnants, button eyes, yarn facial features, and nylon hosiery stuffing.

—Fire-starters from melted candle ends poured over pine cones and dried flower heads in muffin-cup molds.

—Soap: See "Make It" earlier in this chapter.

—Napkin rings: See "Make It" section.

—Make-your-own napkins: Buy some cotton muslin or a big white or light-colored cotton sheet and some fabric crayons. Cut fabric into napkin sizes and edge-stitch. Before Christmas dinner have each person decorate his or her own napkin. Be sure to iron them well to set the dye before sitting down to dinner.

The Day After. To avoid the traditional let down, plan a winter hike to some place where you can build a fire. If there's snow play fox-and-geese. Rather than gathering the gifts and goodies and racing off, savor each other, the gifts, the goodness of friends and relatives. After celebrating God's gift of his Son on Christmas, make this day after Christmas a celebration of God's gift of creation.

❄ FIVE ❄

Fix It

You know what happens when a portrait that has been painted on a panel becomes obliterated through external stains. The artist does not throw away the panel, but the subject of the portrait has to come and sit for it again, and then the likeness is re-drawn on the same material. Even so was it with the All-holy Son of God. He, the Image of the Father, came and dwelt in our midst, in order that He might renew mankind made after Himself....
        —Athanasius, *On the Incarnation*

❄

ONE OF OUR MOST DESTRUCTIVE modern attitudes says that something old and broken should not be repaired but replaced. Thus we throw away an endless stream of things and draw steadily on the resources of creation to replace them.

Several factors contribute to this throwaway attitude. One, of course, is a naive confidence that we will never run out of material to make new things and never run out of places to put the old ones. This attitude was perfected in North America, where the sheer vastness and bounty of the continent encouraged throwaway attitudes that we are only now beginning to be aware of. We have even regarded soil as a throwaway item—there's always more further west—so we mined the soil till it blew away. We have treated water, forests, even animals in the same way. And that picture of nature as an endless, self-renewing cornucopia has shaped our approach to all goods.

Another attitude that has conspired against repair is a prejudice against the old in favor of the new. Till quite recently (and still, for many people), "old-fashioned" was a term of reproach, and words like *up-to-date* and *modern* were all positive. The attitude was given an almost official status by the auto industry, which every year comes out with a new model. (Sometimes that attitude translated into reality, resulting in shoddy workmanship hardly worth repairing.) Thus the illusion of year-by-year progress has influenced our attitude toward technical products.

Yet a third factor contributing to our penchant for replacement rather than repair is the overwhelming need of modern industrial society to find regular buyers for its products. There's no reason why a car shouldn't last twenty years, but if most cars did, then there would be need for far fewer new cars. It is important to keep making cars at least *appear* to be better, so that people with an old model will feel compelled to buy a newer one. A major function of advertising is to convince people that they ought to be good to themselves by buying what's new.

One place where we find this throwaway attitude in modern society is in our attitude toward light bulbs. The new compact fluorescents save about $48 over their lifespan. But we are used to thinking of front-end cost and a steady electric bill that hides the real cost of lighting, so we buy cheap, short-lived light bulbs. (See the section on energy in chapter one, for more on compact fluorescents.)

The Christian has a more fundamental motive to fix rather than replace: God did not make a throwaway creation. Rather, he willed to "fix it." Salvation is the renewing of creation—beginning with men and women, its spoiled stewards. We have misunderstood a "new heaven and a new earth" to mean that God made a throwaway world. We see the Incarnation as God's rescue from the wreck. Rather, it is God's repair work: restoring, renewing, returning (through remade men and women) all created things to their original intention. It is appropriate then as God's stewards that we work not to make "all new things" but rather to make "all things new." And that work begins in our own backyard; in the kitchen, in the car, in using our repair skills and those of others.

FIX IT BY TAKING CARE OF IT

The best way to fix something is to take care of it so that it doesn't break in the first place. This is a principle so obvious it's hardly worth mentioning, yet most of us follow it only haphazardly—partly out of laziness, partly out of ignorance, but largely out of a modern assumption that things ought to work automatically and endlessly without maintenance and without care.

We don't neglect taking care of everything. Prompted by a warranty, we find it easy to see that preventive maintenance gets done on big, expensive things like cars. But even there we often overlook problems that don't result in big cost for us. Since in many cases the car performs slightly better when pollution-control systems are disabled, we don't have strong motives to keep them in repair. Keeping tires aligned and properly inflated prolongs tire life and improves gas mileage, thus reducing the load on the earth's systems. And keeping a car's engine properly tuned is an obvious way to lengthen its life.

Simply keeping a tool cleaned and properly lubricated will greatly prolong its life and efficiency. A little time spent caring for a tool in the proper way will not only prolong its life and efficiency, making repair or replacement unnecessary; it will help us understand and appreciate the qualities of creation that make that tool work. If we never bother to sharpen knives in the first place, we'll never learn the difference between good steel and cheap.

Keeping things sharp is a particular matter of good stewardship. A chain saw with a dull chain will grind ineffectively at the log, producing a pathetic stream of powder instead of big chips of sawdust. The engine and the operator will both overheat, and the saw will wear out faster and likely get discarded as a worthless piece of junk. But a $1.00 file, carefully applied to the teeth at the proper angle, will keep the machine cutting smoothly all day.

We have largely abandoned traditional tools like the crosscut saw in favor of noisy, expensive, and polluting substitutes like the chain saw. Certainly speed and efficiency are reasons. But often our laxity in keeping a tool in shape prompts us to discard an old hand tool in favor of a new power tool that doesn't even work as well. The electric knife—a poor substitute for a good sharp knife—is a good example.

Even more dramatic is the spread of the motorized grass trimmer, which whirls a tough plastic string at a high speed so that it cuts anything in its way. These noisy machines are unquestionably useful in trimming tall weeds or hard-to-get places. But when you're using one you are in a bubble of noise and smell, insulated from the world around you. And the engine overheats and is hard to start, or the starter cord jams, or the monofilament cutter needs replacing or lengthening. Cutting grass with these tools is rarely a pleasant experience.

Contrast that with the elegant tool that it replaces, the scythe. With its sword-like curved blade and handle bent to fit the human body, it is such an impressive cutting tool that it has long been a symbol for death itself, "the grim reaper." Using the scythe is a kind of joy: rhythmic, quiet, you can cut faster than with the noisier machine and use no fuel other than what you ate for breakfast—so long as you stop every so often to touch up the edge with a whetstone or file.

Why then did the scythe go out of style? Probably because of a mistaken notion that it was "old-fashioned" and that the power cutter was a better idea. But probably too because scythes only work well when the blade is very sharp. The electric weed-eater doesn't have to be sharpened, and its unassuming piece of green string seems safer than the three-foot gleaming steel of a scythe. (True, scythes won't cut right up to trees and walls, as well as the filament cutter; for that you'll need to invest in a pair of grass-cutting shears.)

Good hardware or farm-supply stores will have scythes. Or for a catalogue and lots of information about scythes and their care and use, write to The Marugg Company, Tracy City, TN 37387.

Some principles for keeping things in repair:
1. Learn the proper maintenance procedure *before* you use the tool, not after it needs repair.
2. Invest in necessary maintenance equipment—like a file, a whetstone, an oil can.
3. Buy tools that *can* be repaired. Sometimes this costs more, but often not. Sometimes we're trapped into thinking that because we can afford it, we ought to buy the motorized tool rather than its old-fashioned hand-powered equivalent. But the hand tool usually needs far less maintenance and *can be* repaired.
4. See that a tool is cleaned and sharpened when it is put away after the use or the season, rather than left dirty and dull.
5. Establish regular places for tools, and keep them there. This helps prevent deterioration, loss, and breakage.

Once again; these principles of caring for our creation-caring tools are so obvious they're hardly worth mentioning. Yet in listing them we're aware of how far we fall short of even these obvious principles.

One final piece of familial advice. In most families (or

couples or communities), one person will probably be more concerned about maintenance and order than the other. Though the more orderly member needs to be graceful and forgiving, in general his or her concern for keeping things ordered and maintained is a gift that should be honored and imitated: we ought to try to bring our standards *up* to that person's level of concern, rather than let the whole household drop down to the sloppiest level. (Having written this, some of us in this particular household need to go clean up the shop!)

FIX IT BY USING THE SERVICES OF REPAIR PEOPLE

"Fixing" things in the average household requires skills that most of us don't have. So when the leaking pipe, the shorting circuit, and the sticking door exceed our skill, we have three alternatives. The most drastic solution is to "get a new one"—and thus throw away the old.

As we have seen repeatedly, throwing "away" (wherever that is) is usually a bad solution. It is poor stewardship both of the offending thing and of God's creation. But it is a very common solution, as a little back-alley research on garbage day makes clear. Lamps, lawn mowers, sofas, mattresses, chairs, tables, mirrors, backpacks, and tennis rackets regularly appear as fodder for the garbage truck. Sometimes the damage is indeed irreparable, though usually not. But fixing is more bother than nixing: so into the garbage it goes.

This is a pretty radical solution when the offending item is a whole house. But in many cities perfectly good houses are torn down in great numbers and replaced with new ones— often inferior to the old, except that the old ones required some care and repair which no one was prepared to give. Whatever the economic arguments, this kind of expedient destruction is wasteful of both our creations and God's.

A second solution is to use the skills of those who *can* fix things. This is an obvious but underused alternative, and one which in many communities is hardly practiced at all. What we do fix are big, expensive things like TVs, computers, and stereos.

Most large companies have trained servicemen to take care of problems with their own products, and certainly we should avail ourselves of them. But often they are technicians trained with a narrowness necessitated by the complexity of our machines. And often you will be told that the problem cannot be repaired for less money than it would cost you to buy a replacement.

This failure even to try to repair old things is a relatively new development in human society, and one that distances us even further from creation. Till quite recently, there was someone in any community skilled enough to repair our gadgets, usually because he was skilled in *making* the same things. As specialization has increased, the manufacture of the things we use has drawn further and further from ordinary human experience and become more and more complex. Likewise the repair.

Guidelines for a New Tool. Wendell Berry has published some helpful guidelines to help us when we buy a new tool. Here they are:

1. The new tool should be cheaper than the one it replaces.
2. It should be at least as small in scale as the one it replaces.
3. It should do work that is clearly and demonstrably better than the one it replaces.
4. It should use less energy than the one it replaces.
5. If possible, it should use some form of solar energy, such as that of the body.
6. It should be repairable by a person of ordinary intelligence, provided that he or she has the necessary tools.
7. It should be purchasable and repairable as near to home as possible.

8. It should come from a small, privately owned shop or store that will take it back for maintenance and repair.
9. It should not replace or disrupt anything good that already exists, and this includes family and community relationships.[1]

These are good principles for everyone, not just Wendell Berry. If we follow them we will support local shops and repairmen, certainly. But we will also take a second look at the kind of tools we depend on. Perhaps Christians have said yes too easily to every technological innovation and the culture that accompanies it. Perhaps we should take more seriously the example of the Amish, who have kept their technology simple enough so that it is (in Berry's words) "purchasable and repairable as near to home as possible."

The small repairman of clocks and watches, of home appliances, of small motors, the handyman who makes housecalls: they are essential and important parts of the human community, helping us take better care of creation. They are an endangered kind of species and need our support.

We began this "Winter" section of the book with a reflection on the Incarnation and the way it hallows creation, our home, the very nature of human relationships. It is appropriate then that we choose and use our tools in such a way that the extended community of creation and the more immediate communities in which we live are not degraded. That means not only fixing things, but using mainly things that *can be fixed*, by local repair people.

FIX IT BY DEVELOPING YOUR OWN SKILLS

Another possibility, when fixing a thing lies beyond our skill, is to develop the skill to fix it ourselves. There are at least three good reasons for this.

We Won't Throw It away. If we can repair a thing we shouldn't throw it away, with all the cost to creation that entails. A repaired chair or window or waffle iron is a saved one.

We'll Begin to Understand How It Works. To fix something is to begin to understand it. To understand how a plumbing system works is to see a little more deeply into some of the characteristics of creation: the nature of fluids, of gravity, of metals, pressures, and convection. To understand why and how a well-made chair is jointed, braced, and mortised is to see more deeply into the endless possibilities of wood.

One consequence of such deepened knowledge should be praise, as we see ever more deeply into the versatile variety of creation. But another should be better stewardship. To know how a chair is made not only gives us a better understanding of how to care for it; it will help us to distinguish something made poorly from something made well.

Repair Skills Can Be Shared. The third good reason for expanding our skills is that it gives us something to share. A perfected skill is a resource not just for you but for everyone you know. It can be an invitation into a richer human community, in a society longing for community.

Here are some excellent repair resources:
—David Macauley, *The Way Things Work* (Boston: Houghton Mifflin, 1988). This strange and funny book by a great illustrator reduces to visual terms the machines that surround us—from nail clippers to computers. To read the book is to take a cleverly-guided tour through both the inexhaustible qualities of created things and the equally inexhaustible human proclivity for inventing ways to use those qualities.
—*The Reader's Digest Complete Do-It-Yourself Manual* (Pleasantville, NY: The Reader's Digest Association, 1973). A handy-man friend's recommendation: "a satisfying book: once you've bought it, you've got everything."

—*Sunset* Books. A wide variety of well-illustrated, clearly-written books on building, fixing, repairing, remodeling. *Basic Home Repairs Illustrated, Do-It-Yourself Energy-Saving Projects, Bookshelves and Cabinets,* and *Pillows: How to Make* are a few of the books put out by the editors of *Sunset* Magazine, Lane Publishing: Menlo Park, CA.

FIX IT BY MAKING DO

Then, while the Rat busied himself fetching plates, and knives and forks, and mustard which he mixed in an egg cup, the Mole... related—somewhat shyly at first, but with more freedom as he warmed to his subject—how this was planned, and how that was thought out, and how this was got through a windfall from an aunt, and that was a wonderful find and a bargain, and this other thing was bought out of laborious savings and a certain amount of 'going without.'

—Kenneth Grahame, *The Wind in the Willows*

Loren's father was a master at making do. I have fond and exasperated memories of tractors repaired with bits of wire and tin cans, baling wire holding together various household appliances from toilet to furnace, and climbing crampons fashioned from inverted bottle caps on old shoe soles. Loren helped his father with the crampons, a labor of love for his new wife on her first mountain climb. But the bottle caps filled up with ice in the first five minutes of glacier crossing and made more effective skis than crampons.

These aren't examples of the sort to win people over to the virtues of "making do," but they do bear out a bottom line: it helps to be poor and to have lots of imagination. Loren's family was rich in love and good health, in beauty of surroundings and in community life, but they were not rich in money.

The half-dozen chairs in the church lounge had degenerated past the point of general grunginess: the paint was wearing off the arms, the stuffing was leaking out of the upholstery, the nauga-hyde upholstery was fading and discolored. "They've had it," said the committee. "A poor testimony to anyone who comes in the church. Get rid of them."

"Wait a minute," said our friend, as the chairs waited for their trip to outer darkness. "I could fix those and use them."

"Help yourself," said the committee. "It's you or the dump."

So she loaded them in the station-wagon, took them home, started to work. The frames were sound: the chairs weren't going to collapse under anybody. They'd have to be repainted, of course, and re-upholstered. She scraped at the paint on one arm. The wood underneath appeared. It looked like oak. She scraped some more: it *was* oak. No wonder the frames were still sound. She set to work stripping off the old paint: underneath it was all oak, all beautiful. She carefully took off the blotched green plastic upholstery, laid it out on the floor for a pattern, bought textured tan fabric that complemented the oak-grain and traced six new sets of upholstery to enclose the leaking stuffing. Then she spent hours cutting, fitting, sewing, staining the old wood to bring out the grain.

The chairs, their oak arms glowing in the afternoon light, sit in a circle in their home, by windows looking out on the creation which is a tiny bit healthier because the chairs have been saved. Back in the church, the old chairs have been replaced. The church does a good job of presenting the method of salvation: but for people, not usually for chairs.

Making do saves a lot of wear and tear on creation—though maybe not always, in the short run, on the wife! When we come right down to caring for creation in our own backyard, making do is probably the way to begin. In some ways this whole book is about "making do" through such different ways as using two sides of a sheet of paper or making soap from scratch. If consumerism—the need always to buy something new—is one of the biggest threats to creation, then "making do" with what we have is indirectly one of the best ways to care for it.

Living More with Less is the title of a very good book by Doris Janzen Longacre, put out by the Mennonite Central Committee (Scottsdale, PA: Herald Press, 1980). The title is the point of the book—and of this final section in "fixing."

Though we might deny it emphatically, we subconsciously equate quality with quantity. *Always* just one more thing: for one of us, at the moment, it's a Champion juicer; for another it's a really good roto-tiller; for our neighbors it's a matched set of Clydesdale work horses. *Then* we could settle down and live a much richer, fuller, and more environmentally responsible life. And so from one absolute "necessity" to the next, we go on living less with more. To halt the spiral of consuming more and more, we need to start asking ourselves these questions:

—Will this save time, but cut me off from processes that are at the heart of good work?
—Is this just better and bigger? Do I already have something that does the job—or could do it if it were repaired?
—Is this saving me work, but cutting off an opportunity to work shoulder-to-shoulder with friends and strangers?

Wants vs. Needs. Always try to distinguish between what you need and what you want. Be much more cautious about fulfilling your wants.

Resist the temptation to update your possessions to state-of-the-art excellence. The principle applies not only to cars, CD players, and computers, but to camping equipment, gardening and kitchen ware, and energy-saving fluorocompact light bulbs. Though there's no substitute for good tools, it's usually a mistake to think that you need the best tools before you can start taking your work—or your caring for creation—seriously.

Go home and think hard before making any gadget or appliance purchase.

Don't drop hints so friends or relatives know what you want and buy it for you. That's not playing fair. On the other hand, temper care for creation with care for your brothers and sisters. If one of them does give you a new blender, say a genuine thank you and give the old one away.

Wait. Delayed gratification of our wants—and even our needs—develops character and helps us change perspective on which is which. Doing without is almost always good for us.

Remember: buying one thing usually leads to buying another.

Get rid of your charge cards (or make a blood-pact to use them only for identification or *extreme* emergencies). For most of us, credit cards make it entirely too easy to buy something without counting the cost. And lack of money is a good brake to the buying binge.

How to Make Do. Here are some suggestions for learning the art of "making do":

Extended periods of low income are very effective ways of clarifying the difference between needs and wants. So for six months live on half your income; or for one month, live on $25 per person; or see how long you can go without making *any* purchases. (You may be surprised.)

Don't use this or any other "Save the Earth" book as an excuse to buy a whole new set of gadgets and appliances. Use what you have until it's used up and unrepairable. The cost in energy use and toxics in manufacturing and transporting the product will make it hard to justify a new purchase.

Develop a hobby which takes you outside, and whose object is getting to know the inexhaustible variety of creation. Bird-watching; pressing wildflowers; identifying trees, shrubs, and mosses; growing geraniums, gladiolis, or dahlias: these hobbies take a minimum of equipment.

Essential Equipment for "Making Do":
—Perseverance: subtly different from and more important than patience, which may actually hinder the process, as adrenalin is a real help in a pinch.
—A committed spouse: anyone who is not tied to you by the tie that sometimes gags and binds could not possibly stick with you through the thick and thin of making do!

SIX

Share It

When I was at school my jography told as th' world was shaped like a orange an' I found out before I was ten that th' whole orange doesn't belong to nobody. No one owns more than his bit of a quarter an' there's times it seems like there's not enow quarters to go round. But don't you—none o' you—think as you own th' whole orange or you'll find out you're mistaken, an' you won't find it out without hard knocks.

—Susan Sowerby, in Frances Hodgson Burnett, *The Secret Garden*

I T'S HARD TO TALK ABOUT SHARING nowadays without someone giving a condescending smile. Perhaps when we were young we were told too often, "Share your toys," and now that we're grown up we are approached too often by one charity or another, whether in the form of a glossy letter or an outstretched hand on the street.

"Donor fatigue" seems to be a phenomenon of the nineties: the identified (and thus somehow acceptable) response of the wealthy to the overwhelming needs of the poor. And we've witnessed the dubious success—or outright failure—of government programs that enforce sharing, whether through foreign aid or welfare, and have settled comfortably back into affirmations of the sanctity of ownership.

We've got it wrong, of course, and a book on caring for

creation is a good occasion, once more, to try to set things right. What we call ownership is really *stewardship* of some little bit of creation. C.S. Lewis' "Screwtape" gives a hell's-eye view of the matter. After making fun of the human penchant for attaching "my" to everything from boots to dogs to wives to God, the devilish narrator observes:

> And all the time the joke is that the word "Mine" in its fully possessive sense cannot be uttered by a human being about anything. In the long run either Our Father [Satan] or the Enemy [God] will say "Mine" of each thing that exists.... At present the Enemy says "Mine" of everything on the pedantic, legalistic ground that He made it: Our Father hopes in the end to say "Mine" of all things on the more realistic and dynamic ground of conquest....[1]

The beauty of the word *creation* (rather than alternatives like *nature, environment,* or *natural resources*) is that we can hardly utter it without being reminded that "the earth is the Lord's" and that "it is he who made us, and not we ourselves." In that context sharing takes on a more radical meaning, less redolent of nursery school platitudes and political soft-heartedness. We are reminded that our very existence is the result of the Creator's sharing.

Which returns us (as the Bethlehem stable ought) to the humdrum of "our own backyard"—or more specifically, our back *fence* or whatever we erect, really or symbolically, to separate ourselves from our neighbors. Winter in general and Christmas in particular is a good (and traditional) time to lower those barriers, to recognize the life we share. And it is a good time to reflect on some specific ways of sharing that not only deepen our sense of the human community but also deepen our sense of the life we share with the earth itself. The central biblical teaching here for us is in Philippians 2: "Each of you should look not only to your own interests, but also to the interests of others. Your attitude should be the same as that of Christ Jesus: Who, being in very nature God, did not consider equality with God something to be grasped, but made himself nothing, taking the very nature of a servant..." (Phil 2:4-7).

We can be servants to each other—and indirectly, to creation itself by sharing tools, skills, meals, and books.

SHARE TOOLS

Near the end of March, 1845, I borrowed an axe and went down to the woods by Walden Pond, nearest to where I intended to build my house, and began to cut down some tall, arrowy white pines, still in their youth, for timber. It is difficult to begin without borrowing, but perhaps it is the most generous course thus to permit your fellow-men to have an interest in your enterprise. The owner of the axe, as he released his hold on it, said it was the apple of his eye; but I returned it sharper than I received it.

—Henry David Thoreau, *Walden*

They went to the Jordan and began to cut down trees. As one of them was cutting down a tree, the iron axe-head fell into the water. "Oh , my lord," he cried out, "it was borrowed!" —2 Kings 6:4-5

Shortly after the first tool was invented it was surely borrowed. History does not record whether it was returned sharper than it was lent—or was lost. Whatever the case, humanity is both a tool-making and a tool-borrowing species. We have reason to be ambivalent about both characteristics. The tools we make—from stone axe to chain saw, from digging stick to bulldozer, from spear to jet plane—enormously extend our powers. Those powers can be used for the good of creation or for destruction.

Tool-borrowing is likewise two-sided. The more skill we have, the more we love our tools and hate to see them misused. Nevertheless, borrowing is a way not only of testing

and strengthening friendships, but of sharing our stewardship of creation.

As I write this section on tools Mary Ruth calls me to
our bedroom window to look at the *Pacific Swift*, an
eighty-foot schooner, heading under full sail up Trin-
comali Channel between Saltspring and Galiano Islands.
It is a beautiful sight, carrying its many tons and passengers along on a blustery south wind. We rarely see so
large a sailing ship, and even the small ones are usually
bare-masted, chugging along before even a following
wind on the loud, smelly dependability of their engines.

The *Swift* (which was built for a Christian sail training
organization, and which regularly crosses oceans with its
crew and thirty trainees) had its ribs built here on
Galiano; then the ship itself was built in 1986 at Vancouver's EXPO—all under the watchful eyes and hands
of Greg Foster, a Galiano Island shipwright. He continues to build wooden boats at his small boatyard on
Whaler Bay on the south end of the island. To work
there is a rich privilege: partly because of the scent of
pine tar, yellow cedar, and Douglas fir, but largely because of the deliberate peace and pace of the place, the
quiet intensity of careful work.

Almost all of the work is done with hand tools: not in
order to be quaint or purist, but because for this work
nothing is better. The basic tools needed for building a
boat like the *Swift* can be carried under one arm—
though the skills for using them are almost forgotten.
When I took a woodworker friend to the shop not long
ago, he was impressed, and rode back up the island in
silence. "I thought I needed a lot of equipment to do
good work," he said. "But he does all that with just a few
hand tools. It changes the way I think about tools."

Some tools are small and relatively inexpensive; those are the kind that every household should own. But others are large and expensive, and provide good opportunities for us to learn the difficult lessons of sharing.

No one can tell you which tools you ought to own and which you ought to buy in common; that will vary with your needs, your skill, and your neighbors. It's worth reflecting for a moment on the fact that there are really two kinds of tools: tools for fixing other tools (that is, machines) and tools for working with created materials themselves (mainly wood).

Pliers, wrenches, and screwdrivers are tools for tools; and they are quite neccessary in the machine-surrounded environment we have built for ourselves. Such tools need little skill or practice to learn to operate or maintain, but they often require a great deal of knowledge about the complex mechanism being worked on, whether it's a toaster or a TV set.

The other kind of tool—such things as chisels, planes, saws—require more skill for operation, but on the whole less knowledge. A man can carve an eagle out of wood with a sharp knife and no more knowledge than what an eagle looks like; but the skills he needs for the carving have taken years to develop. It's hard to function in the modern world without tools to fix our tools with, but we should not neglect the older tools for shaping creation directly—and the skill to use them well.

Here are some suggestions for tools to own and tools to share:

Tools You Need in Your Home:
—Hammer.
—Pliers.
—Screwdriver(s). Buying screwdrivers was easier when there was only one kind of screw head. Unless you do a lot of repair work, the clever screwdriver with interchangeable points that store in the handle is a good investment.

—One or two *good* adjustable wrenches. An adjustable or crescent wrench is never quite as good as a one-sized wrench for any particular job. Again, if you're doing a lot of mechanical repairs, you'll want a set of "end" wrenches or a socket set. That begins to get expensive, and perhaps into the "tools to share" category. But if you borrow wrench sets, take care to keep track of and return all the parts.

—Pipe-wrench: If you need one, you probably need two.

—Hand saw.

—Plane: large and small, for doors and drawers that won't fit and for smoothing wood.

—Drawknife or spokeshave: a neglected tool consisting of a sharp blade with two handles, ideal for shaping wood.

—Vise: for holding wood if you're going to use a plane or drawknife.

—Whetstone or oil stone: for keeping cutting tools sharp.

—Drill and appropriate bits: The old "brace" or hand drill is remarkably effective. But buy your own power drill if you really are going to drill a lot of holes.

—Basic garden tools: shovel, hoe, rake.

—Axe: If you use a lot of firewood and have access to large logs, you'll also want a heavier splitting maul and at least one wedge.

Tools to Share:

—Power saw or "Skil-saw": hand held.

—Table or radial arm saw: one or the other; the argument over which is best will never be settled.

—Propane torch: useful as a soldering iron—especially with copper pipe—and whenever you need controlled, intense heat.

—Lawn mower: These can quite happily be shared. Unless you have a very large lawn, don't invest in a power mower. A good hand mower (they're almost as expensive) is relatively trouble-free and easier to move from house to house. Aside from the near silence, they provide good exercise and are much more maneuverable. They also need to be sharpened more regularly, since they depend less on brute force for cutting.

—Pruning saw(s) and clipper(s).

—Chain saw.

Both lists could go on and on. The point is to have tools that enable you to carefully tend and use the garden of creation—and to be willing to share them. Access to good tools makes you able to use creation more responsibly. But good tools also enable you to do more damage: both to yourself and the rest of creation. So tools without knowledge are worse than worthless.

Good tools are not cheap, which is one reason why you should consider sharing them. But sharing can cause no end of problems.

Some Principles to Guide Sharing:

1. Better than common ownership (which compromises stewardship) is an arrangement in which different people buy tools that they then agree to share. The owner continues to be particularly responsible for ongoing maintenance, and the tool "lives" at his or her house.
2. The borrower always is responsible for replacing or repairing lost or broken items—unless the thing is something that regularly wears out and needs replacing, in which case the best arrangement is to divide the cost.
3. "Good fences make good neighbors" (according to Robert Frost). So do return tools. Return the tool promptly, clean, and at least as sharp as it was when you borrowed it.

SHARE SKILLS

We can share tools; but more fundamentally, we can share ourselves and our own skills. Creation is too much for us to know, even those aspects of it that we encounter every day.

We suffer from the increasing individualism and specialization of our society, which distances us from the processes that turn creation into things for our use. Thus it is easy for us to use those things carelessly.

Much is gained when we do things together. The "barn-raising" was an emblem of cooperation in communities, but it is only one of a number of communal activities that have shaped societies since prehistoric times: the hunt, the harvest, the quilting party. We probably romanticize these things, and we could not return to them even if we wanted to. But they are examples of community activities in which two things were accomplished: community members reaffirmed their connectedness to each other and to the cycles of creation that nourished them; and skills for dealing with creation were passed on to the younger members of the community.

Here are some possibilities for sharing skills today:

Canning and Preserving. This shortcuts the commercial preservation process that has resorted to the use of preservatives and colorings, in order to process fruits grown with pesticides and herbicides. Most people lack the equipment, skills, or space to begin to preserve their own food. But the project becomes less daunting if people who know what they're doing take charge.

In canning season, find someone who knows these skills (she's likely to be an older woman who thinks her skills old-fashioned and worthless). Pick your peaches or beans or apples, then find a church or community kitchen and make applesauce, peach jam, or whatever the crop dictates. In the process everyone will learn something, and you'll have confidence that you're eating good food.

Community Gardening. Especially in urban areas, many communities are finding ways of using vacant lots—whether old railroad right-of-ways, unused building sites, or the space around apartment buildings—for shared gardens. This is good for all sorts of reasons (see chapter seven, "Planting"), but not the least of them is that it gives members of a community—especially older members—a chance to pass on essential skills to others.

Sharing Knowledge. Many of us have taken it upon ourselves to get to know one aspect of creation well, whether it be wildflowers, birds, the geology of a particular area, or making things with stone, wood, wool, clay, or leather. Look for people in your neighborhood or church who have this knowledge, and ask them to teach a group. This deepens our knowledge of creation and each other, and is a good way of bringing Christians and non-Christians together around one thing they share: a love of creation. Such times can often open doors to a deeper knowledge of the Creator.

SHARE MEALS

> *The metaphor for the planetary community, to replace the old image of men on horseback riding around the planet keeping us all in order, may be that of the family at the dinner table: the world family at the world dinner table. The family at the table is a basic human metaphor of sharing.*
>
> —Dr. Elise Boulding "The Place of the Family in Times of Social Transition" (Lecture at the University of British Columbia)

You prepare a table before me....   —Psalm 23:5

Creation is a banquet to which we are invited by the Creator. The Bible is full of God's invitation to taste his goodness: and that goodness is often offered or symbolized in things to eat, from the roasted lamb of the Passover to the bread and wine of Jesus' Last Supper. Meals for human beings are never just "feedings": even the simplest is a ceremony, a communion. In meals we sample the infinite variety of God's gifts; in meals also we inevitably are nourished by the life of another creature.

In this section we describe a variety of meals which are occasions for communion with each other and with the Creator, and which provide ways of reflecting on the fact that every meal is, indeed, a table spread before us by the Creator himself.

A MEAL AT THE WORLD'S DINNER TABLE

The first meal we describe here reflects this larger struggle in sharing the world's dinner table. This is a good meal to have with a study group, a youth group, or a class. Everybody has fun, but everyone also goes away with quite a vivid picture of several aspects of how our eating affects creation.

—First, the vast discrepancies between the way the majority of the world eats and the way we North Americans eat;
—Second, the high energy cost of the North American diet. Chinese agriculture, for example, produces about twenty-five calories for every calorie expended; American agriculture *uses* over two calories to produce a calorie of food energy. See discussion of animal protein in chapter eight, page 175, for more on the energy input into our food;
—Third, the considerable squandering of resources our diet involves;
—Fourth, the good and nourishing food we could still have if we changed our eating habits—food, in fact, that would be considerably better for us. (See more about food in the "Eating" chapters of "Spring.")

The Meal:
This is a very structured potluck, with recipes distributed beforehand and the food prepared by the participants. The

people are divided proportionately, and given packets of
"Energy Units [E.U's]" with which to "buy" their food from a
central "smorgasbord" table. (Each piece of paper in the
packet is worth ten E.U's, so "Americans" get ten pieces,
"East Indians" two, etc.) "Energy Units" refer to the estimated energy cost of one serving of the food. For example,
beef takes far more energy to produce than rice does, and a
coke with its aluminum can is more expensive than without
the can. (One "Energy Unit" represents about fifty watts, or
forty-three calories; remember, the number measures what
the food takes to produce, not the energy it yields when you
eat it.) As in the real world, about ten percent of the people
have the choice of eating very energy-expensive foods; the
rest have less freedom, and at least twenty-five percent have
to choose their food very carefully—but can still eat a nourishing meal. If possible, people should know their "national-
ity" a few hours or days in advance, to have some time to
think about what their possible approach to the meal will be.
Foreign aid, charity, conquest, and hostage-taking can all
happen—though the meal does not depend on those she-
nanigans.

People draw lots to choose what country they will represent, and once the tickets are issued, the residents of each
country are welcome to head over to the buffet. Americans,
naturally, are first; residents of India are last.

The Guests:

U.S.A. *(representing North American, Australia)*	10%	100 E.U.
England *(representing Europe, Russia)*	20%	70 E.U.
Japan *(representing China, the wealthy Orient)*	25%	40 E.U.
Honduras *(representing Latin America, parts of Africa)*	20%	30 E.U.
India *(representing poorer Orient, parts of Africa)*	25%	20 E.U.

The Tables. Set a different table for each country, trying to
match the settings with the country. India could have a

bright Indian tablecloth and plates but (in keeping with Indian custom) no utensils. The table settings should not point out contrasts of wealth and poverty (that will become plain enough when the food appears) so much as to display the rich diversity of each culture.

The Menu. (Page references are to the Mennonite Central Committee's *More with Less Cookbook* by Doris Janzen Longacre—now into its 36th printing. The ingredients in parentheses are the main source of protein in each dish.)

60	Roast Beef
55	Skillet Beef with Lentils p. 107 (meat, lentils, rice)
54	Lasagna—any standard recipe with meat (meat, wheat, cheese)
48	Chicken-Cheese Casserole p. 124 (chicken, cheese, bread)
24	Fried Chicken
23	Sweet and Sour Soybeans p. 113 (soybeans, rice)
22	Soybean Pie p. 111 (soybeans, cornmeal, cheese)
20	Lasagna Roll-Ups p. 119 (wheat, cheese)
20	Oatmeal Cake (with topping) p. 285 (oats, wheat, nuts)
18	Potato Filling p. 233 (potatoes, egg, bread)
17	Pop can (empty—refund value)
15	Blue Cheese Dressing—store-bought (milk, egg, cheese, oil)
12	Kusherie p. 108 (rice, lentils)
11	Pop (without can)
10	Cooked Carrots
10	Rice
8	Salad—lettuce, carrots, onion, celery, without dressing
8	High-Protein Rolls p. 64 (wheat, cheese, eggs)
7	Carribean Rice and Beans p. 103 (rice, beans)
7	Banana
7	Orange
6	Curried Split Peas (Dhal) p. 135 (peas)

6   Whole Wheat Peanut-butter Cookies p. 289 (wheat, peanuts, egg, milk)

5   Garden Vegetable Curry p. 134—let sauce boil down at the very end so the curry can be eaten with bread (potatoes, beans)

5   Whole Wheat Rolls p. 64 (milk, eggs, wheat)

4   Parsley Dressing p. 247—skip the avocado

4   Local Organically-grown Apple

4   Chapatis p. 84

A Meal for the World

> *Is not this the kind of fasting I have chosen:*
>   *to loose the chains of injustice*
>   *and untie the cords of the yoke,*
>   *to set the oppressed free*
>   *and break every yoke?*
> *Is it not to share your food with the hungry*
>   *and to provide the poor wanderer with shelter—*
> *when you see the naked, to clothe him....*
>   —Isaiah 58:6-8

Give up a meal a week and give the cost of that meal to a world relief program. In this way you can share, in a very small way, the hunger of many in the world and give your meal to those who need it.

In Matthew's Gospel Jesus says that serving something to a hungry stranger is serving him (see Mt 25:37,40). But meals with strangers can be awkward and uncomfortable. How do we get past the superficial chit-chat of "where do you live?" and "what do you do?" We'd rather feed strangers long-distance through a contribution to world relief. One of our friends frequently takes street people who beg for money to a restaurant and treats them to a more nourishing meal than they would buy with a gift of money. That's a good idea.

Here are two suggestions for more structured meals with strangers.

Ask people home for coffee after church. When we spent a year in the Dutch Christian Reformed Community in Michigan, we appreciated very much the convention of asking a handful of people home for coffee and sweet breads after church. It's simple, not so daunting as a dinner, and gives a good chance to "break bread" with people in church.

Invite a few people whom you don't know very well—and who don't know each other—to help you make a meal. A homemade meal of pasta (with everybody getting their hands floury turning out the fettucini) and churned ice cream (with everybody taking turns at the crank) is an excellent way for people to get to know each other. By the time you sit down to eat together, you'll have become friends through simply working together, turning God's gifts of creation into something to eat.

A Meal with Friends

Jesus said to them, "Come and have breakfast." None of the disciples dared ask him, "Who are you?" They knew it was the Lord. Jesus came, took the bread and gave it to them, and did the same with the fish. —John 21:12-13

We're all terribly busy these days; a full date book is the modern status symbol. The God of creation, however, shames our priorities. Jesus took time not only to serve but also to *make* breakfast for his friends. And in the talk there on the beach over bread and fried fish, Jesus tells Peter, "If you love me, feed my sheep."

Peter was the disciple who always wanted to do great and glorious deeds: walk on water and build monuments. When he saw the resurrected Jesus, his mind must have throbbed with plans and possibilities. But Jesus brought him down to earth by feeding him and telling him to feed others.

Of course, more than food is on the agenda here. Jesus wanted Peter to get back on track after his three-time denial. The message was—and is—"Start with basics." So often in all our causes and concerns, our courting of influential people and business ties, we are too busy for friends. But meals with good friends give us chances to share ideas and concerns for both daily life and our care for creation. And friends will, as Jesus did for Peter, bring us down to earth and keep us on track.

If you don't have time to make a meal (as Jesus did!) try a "Lazy Susan" meal. This kind of meal has many possibilities. The host provides the basic food; the guests bring the toppings. Put the toppings on a Lazy Susan (a big rotating platter) or any tray in the middle of the table, and have a good meal.

Breakfast is a neglected and good meal to have with friends. Everybody should be free if you start it early enough. There are usually duties that give an automatic end to the time, removing the need for worrying about when to go home. And there are so many good things to eat for breakfast!

Here are menus for two breakfasts and a dinner with friends.

The host provides	*The guests provide*
Waffles	butter, yogurt, whipped cream, syrup, chopped nuts, fruit toppings
Crepes	Peaches cut up, apples cut up, blueberries, strawberries, raspberries, blackberries, whipped cream, nuts, powdered sugar, cinnamon
Tortillas	hamburger, refried beans, sour cream, avocados, onions, lettuce, tomatoes

A Meal Alone

Here I am! I stand at the door and knock. If anyone hears my voice and opens the door, I will come in and eat with him and he with me. —Revelation 3:20

Many of us eat quite a few meals alone: not only hurried breakfasts and preoccupied lunch breaks, but evening meals as well. Traditionally evening is a time to share not only food but also our thoughts, the day's highs and lows, with others. It is a time for mutual encouragement, for what we often call "touching base" with someone else.

Each meal alone may seem to symbolize, even shout, our *loneliness*. But no meal need be *all* alone. Consider making each meal a celebration of creation. Invite creation—creatures of beauty, nature, sustenance to join you.

Grace the table or tray with a flower. Put on some quiet music. Don't plop your food on your plate; decorate your plate. This doesn't need to be a long job. If you have window herbs, a sprig of basil or three chives may be all that's needed. Both creation and Creator will be present.

Which brings us back around to the dining room. This room says, in effect, that the common, daily, and necessary business of eating is just that—common, daily, and necessary—but that it is also a picture of the thing that lies at the root of all life; namely, the principle of exchange. My Life For Yours. We enact that principle whenever we assemble and sit down at the table. We may be sitting down to cornflakes, pizza, or Beluga caviar, but whatever it is, life has been laid down for us. We are receiving life by chewing and swallowing the life of something else. We have to do it to stay alive. We have to do it daily. As long as we live, we will be doing it. Nothing could be more ordinary and functional. But there it is— the biggest mystery of all, right there before us, three times a day. We are enacting the rite. We are participating in the holy mystery.

—Thomas Howard, *Splendor in the Ordinary* (Wheaton, IL: Tyndale House Publishers, 1976), 66. Republished as *Hallowed Be This House*.

Some Good Books on Meals and Sharing Them:
Bread for the World, Revised Edition, Arthur Simon.
Celebrate the Feast: Celebrate the Old Testament in Your Own Home or Church, Martha Zimmerman. A book for celebration of the traditional feasts in the Old Testament where

the meals are the message.

Extending the Table: A World Community Cookbook, Joetta Handrich Schlaback. Recipes and stories in the spirit of *More-with-Less.*

For the Life of the World: Sacraments and Orthodoxy, Alexander Schmemann. A profound study of the meaning of the Lord's Supper for our life as creatures made in God's image.

The Supper of the Lamb: A Culinary Reflection, Robert Farrar Capon. A wise, humorous, and theologically deep consideration of the meaning of cooking and eating.

SHARE BOOKS

> *"... I am gathering words.*
> *For the winter days are long and many*
> *and we'll run out of things to say."*
> —Leo Lionni, *Frederick*

Reading books is an important way to care for creation, so we'd like to talk about books in two ways: first, to say a few things about reading in general; second, to suggest a handful of good books—most of them stories—that embody good attitudes toward creation. There are many good books on "the environment," but the ones we've listed here—for all ages—are more than environmental books: they're stories and novels that show us people discovering, struggling with, and *living* the mystery of what it means to be a creature.

Like many things, books are better shared: both by telling a person about good books you've read and by reading aloud together. This last habit, ideally practiced around the fire in the dark days of winter, keeps alive one of the most ancient of human activities: the telling of stories. Stories help to tell us who and why we are. It's no accident that God's word is communicated to us mainly in stories: narratives of real people who loved, fought, disobeyed, and worshiped. Stories are thus good ways to discover who we are and what we ought to be doing in creation.

Unfortunately, we live in a society that reads less and less. The main reason for this effective illiteracy—even among the highly educated—is television. Though the medium had great promise, it has failed miserably and exists mainly for the purpose of selling products. In its role of shaping human creatures into voracious consumers in a throwaway culture, TV shares, with the automobile, the honor of the most destructive of twentieth-century inventions.

TV or not, reading is valuable both for the stories it gives us and for the way it exercises our imaginations. It is valuable too because it comes uninterrupted by attempts to sell us something. It is the ideal creation-friendly entertainment, its only cost being the paper it's printed on, only a tiny fraction of the paper used for newspapers and packaging. But even those are minor reasons. The real reason to read books, and share them, is the worlds they open up. Here are a handful of good stories about creatures in creation that will give you and your children more to be human with.

Picture Books for Children:

Barbara Cooney, *Miss Rumphius.* A little girl is told that the one thing she must do is make the world more beautiful. She finally discovers how she can do it: by planting lupines.

Lindee Climo, *Chester's Barn.* A loving look at the inhabitants of a Prince Edward Island farm.

Virginia Burton, *The Little House.* A little house in the country is slowly enclosed by a busy city—till a boy who grew up there finds it and moves it out to the country again.

Mike Mulligan and His Steam Shovel. An outmoded man and his outmoded machine find new jobs.

Robert McCloskey, *Time of Wonder.* A wonderful book about a summer on an island, which is a microcosm of the whole rich world of creation.

Graham Greene, *The Little Train; The Little Fire Engine*, illustrated by Edward Ardizzoni. Two books about outmoded, discarded engines that lack love and affection. These books—and *Mike Mulligan*—all help us at least to think twice about the littered road to "progress."

Donald Hall, *The Oxcart Man*, illustrated by Barbara Cooney. The Oxcart Man and his family live their lives around the seasons of the year.

Catharine Gardam, *The Animals' Christmas*, illustrated by Gavin Rowe. On Christmas Eve the animals steal away from the farm for their own Christmas, singing with the angels. A beautiful reminder of a restored creation in which all creatures praise their Creator.

Elsa Beskow, *Children of the Forest*, illustrated by the author and adapted from the Swedish. The story of a forest family of little people. The children collect berries and mushrooms for the winter, and cotton grass for weaving into rugs. They learn the language of the wind and every kind of tree from Owl. They work hard, play long, and obviously love their forest life.

Dr. Seuss, *The Lorax*. The classic environmental fable, funny and sad, about the damage done by "biggering and biggering"—and about the Lorax, "who speaks for the trees."

Bill Peet, *The Wump World*. The Wumps are invaded by the Pollutias who have used up their old planet Pollutus and moved on to this new world.

Nick Butterworth and Mick Inkpen, *Wonderful Earth!* The story of creation and a plea to care for it, with wildly wonderful "activity" illustrations. It shows a world we can change from a sad, polluted earth face to a glad, cared-for face. Makes the point!

All of these last three books are a little heavy-handed—as are many recent books for children on environmental subjects. A few such books (try to keep them very few) are probably justifiable in the world we live in. But keep the balance on the side of joy—in books like *Miss Rumphius* and *Time of Wonder.*

Stories for Older Children:

C.S. Lewis, *The Magician's Nephew.* All the Narnia books are good, but this one especially because of its picture of creation as a response to the Creator's song.

Kenneth Grahame, *The Wind in the Willows.* The incomparable story of animals in an English wood who combine the characteristics of real animals with all the foibles of human beings entering the technical age.

Frances Hodgson Burnett, *The Secret Garden.* Three children discover a long-neglected garden, which becomes a place of physical and spiritual healing.

T.H. White, *The Sword in the Stone.* This first part of *The Once and Future King,* White's telling of the Arthurian story, shows Merlin educating the young Arthur by turning him into a falcon, a fish, an ant, and various other creatures.

T.H. White, *Mistress Masham's Repose.* An unjustly neglected story about a lonely, imaginative girl who discovers a group of Lilliputians brought back two hundred years ago on the ship that rescued Gulliver. This book is wonderfully, wisely attuned to the created world and to our tendency to confuse might with right.

For Adults (but good to read aloud to older children):

J.R.R. Tolkien, *The Lord of the Rings* (also *The Hobbit,* which can be read to younger children). Few books have done so much to waken people to the beauty of creation as this massive (and deeply Christian) myth about the struggle of defenseless good against evils that would destroy the earth.

Richard Adams, *Watership Down* and *The Plague Dogs.* These are great, deep adventure stories about talking animals who are fully animal, struggling to cope with an increasingly threatening human world.

C.S. Lewis, *That Hideous Strength*. One of Lewis' greatest and most prophetic books: about an attempt to establish Hell on earth in the name of progress and efficiency. This sounds more familiar today than when Lewis wrote it almost fifty years ago.

John Steinbeck, *The Grapes of Wrath*. Steinbeck's greatest novel, about the misuse of land and people in the depression years. It is set in the American southwest and structured by parallels with the Israelite exodus to the Promised Land.

Margaret Craven, *I Heard the Owl Call My Name*. A young Anglican priest learns to live and die in the wild beauty of a remote Indian village on the British Columbia Coast.

Frank Herbert, *Dune*. One of the reasons the first Dune novel became so popular (its many sequels never quite measured up) is because of its astonishingly powerful recreation of a world where water is a rarity. It popularized the idea of the ecology of a whole planet and the possibility of changing it. It remains a thought-provoking science-fiction novel.

Paul Willis, *No Clock in the Forest*. A wonderful romance, echoing both Chaucer and Lewis, about good and evil creatures in a world very much like the West Coast Cascade Mountains. A funny, profound, and deeply Christian myth, which has been called an "eco-fantasy."

Nonfiction about the Created World:

Annie Dillard, *Pilgrim at Tinker Creek*. A Job-like meditation on the intricacy, beauty, and terror of creation.

Aldo Leopold, *Sand County Almanac*. This book is one of the main sources of the "environmental movement," written with a poet's sensitivity and an ecologist's understanding.

We need to learn and live its wisdom in Christian ways.

Edward Abbey, *Desert Solitaire.* A profound appreciation of the desert, written with a lyrical, bitter brilliance by a person angry at what he perceives to be Christendom's degradation of creation.

Barry Lopez, *Crossing Open Ground.* A contemporary naturalist writes these essays out of a Christian sensitivity to the carelessness of our relationship with creation.

Wendell Berry, *What Are People For; Home Economics; The Unsettling of America; Collected Poems.* These eloquent essays and poems by a Kentucky farmer and poet prophesy our unwise course in our relationship to the earth, to ourselves, and to our Creator.

PART THREE

SPRING

Things to Do

❀ Dig deep down into the richness of life: plant a garden.

❀ Brew a batch of compost tea to feed your garden.

❀ Concoct a compost blender stew to feed your plants.

❀ Keep weeds down and moisture in with much mulch.

❀ Save water with soaker hoses, drip irrigation and night watering.

❀ If you live in the city, plant a window or porch garden.

❀ Landscape your lawn with edibles.

❀ Learn how to save your own seeds.

❀ Preserve genetic diversity by growing some older, non-hybrid varieties each year.

❀ Plant for the future with native tree species.

❀ Fight to preserve old trees and forests.

❀ Take joy in planting a flower garden for birds or butterflies, OR for rich fragrance or evening enjoyment.

❀ Help wildness live on, sow seeds of local native flowers and shrubs.

❀ Increase your delight in the glory of gardening by reading about the intricate diversity of growing things.

❀ Buy meat, eggs, and milk products from sources that treat animals humanely.

❀ Eat more poultry and grains for protein sources.

❀ Use meat for FLAVORING the main course rather than as THE main course.

❀ Rediscover the lowly potato as a good, reliable food.

❀ Support your local farmer's market.

❀ Get to know some local farmers who will let you buy or u-pick directly from them.

❀ Read the labels to avoid unnecessary and questionable additives and preservatives.

❀ Make your own ready-made meals: when you make a soup, stew, or casserole, double the amount and freeze the leftovers for next week.

❀ Preserve and protect small wild areas.

❀ Learn where your water comes from and where your waste water goes.

❀ Preserve small farms and communities; help keep alive a respect and appreciation for their role in preserving the stability of agriculture AND culture.

❀ Stay married and work with your family to care for creation.

❀ Take regular walks with your children to keep in touch with the world of creation in "your own backyard."

Spring and Resurrection

Who would have thought my shrivel'd heart
Could have recovered greennesse?
—George Herbert, "The Flower"

WE DO NOT KNOW IN WHICH season the first Christmas took place, but we have a pretty good idea of the time of Jesus' death and resurrection. It was at the time of the Jewish Passover, which is always in the spring. This can be a profound reminder of the inescapable miracle of creation, and its dependence on "the lamb slain before the foundation of the world."

In the increasingly manmade world where most of us live, it becomes easier and easier for us to ignore the seasons. Given cold in the winter, heat in the summer, and storms in the fall, there are lots of apparently civilized reasons to live in a world where seasons and weather have little impact. So we have managed to insulate ourselves rather well from the fact that we are creatures, living in a wild and gorgeous creation not of our own making.

Thus one value of spring. Even in the city (especially in the north, after months of gray and cold) there comes a moment when we see the unexpected purple of a crocus, or sniff the scent of grass, or hear birdsong. In that instant we know that our world is bigger, stranger, and more beautiful than anything humans can make.

So springtime, when the processes of life and rejuvenation are proceeding at a dramatic pace, is a good time for us to reflect on the details of our own participation in what Gerard Manley Hopkins called "all this juice and all this joy." Our dependence on the cycles of rejuvenation that sustain earth, air, water, and live things is easier to see in the spring, and harder to ignore. And the regular miracle of an opening leaf or a hatching egg—multiplied a billionfold across the landscape—makes us think of the greatest miracle of restored life that we celebrate at Easter, on which all the other miracles rest.

It is a good time too to reflect on the fragility of those same processes and on the awesome power we have to disrupt them. Significantly, the book that probably did more than anything else to waken the world to the damage we do was *Silent Spring* by Rachel Carson. She wrote of the ominous shadow cast by the increasing presence of chemicals in the circles of the biosphere, and the possibility that we might, through indiscriminate pesticide use, close down that miracle sometime in the future. Her worries were not unfounded. Though we have reduced or eliminated some of the problem chemicals she wrote about more than thirty years ago, we have introduced others, and are still engaging in a rapid (though largely uinintentional) depletion of the habitat for wild things.

Spring is a reminder both of the beauty of creation and its fragility. The threat of a "silent spring" challenges us to care for creation and daunts us with the bigness of the task, the stubbornness of our misdoing. But it is also the time of Easter, and thus a reminder of the extent to which the Creator has gone to care for creation. And from that care, extended to us and the whole cosmos, we can draw both strength and joy for the task of tending the garden God has given us to work.

SEVEN

Planting

When Mary Magdalene
Saw Christ at dawn
In the tomb-haunted grove
She thought he was the gardener,

Then saw he was the Christ
But still she was mistaken,
Not seeing that the flowers in the rock,
The grass, the gnarled, deep-rooted olive trees
The rock itself
Were rooted in his flesh
And nourished by his blood.

For Christ was gardener of that place
But hid his workman's hands,
The flowers of his flesh,
Lest the young church see
Persephone, Osiris, or only wild Pan
And not the God beyond the world
Who made it for our flesh, and his:
And tends, in each new Adam,
The garden of his earth.

—Loren Wilkinson

TWO GARDENS, EDEN AND GETHSEMANE, frame the human story. Eden stands at the beginning. It has come to be almost a synonym for perfect creation: creation at rest, creation without sin. The Garden of Gethsemane was also, we can assume, a place of peace and rest. It was a favorite haunt of Jesus and his disciples, and when Jesus went there on the night of his betrayal the disciples promptly fell asleep.

Yet in the goodness of these gardens occurred the greatest degradations of God: one, in Eden, warped and wounded our relationship to the Creator; the other, in Gethsemane, set in motion the escalating horrors of wounds to the Creator himself. The one wound brought death to the world; the other brought death to the Son of God—and life to the world.

A third garden is less well-known as a garden because its central feature was a tomb. Here God the Son was buried. The three days of burial had quenched in the disciples any hope that the death of their friend was not final or real. Mary Magdalene, when she saw the tomb empty, didn't throb with hope; she assumed that someone had moved the body. She mourned her fallen Messiah as a Man among men, but certainly not as the Creator. When she saw Jesus she mistook him for a gardener. And so the central acclamation of Easter—the good news that life has conquered death—comes to a weeping woman in a garden.

That these roots of salvation history are sunk in the soil of gardens is no accident. The mystery and the particular matter and manner in which God shows his meanings are one. Jesus himself described God's central mystery by using the manner of a seed: "The hour has come for the Son of Man to be glorified. I tell you the truth, unless a kernel of wheat falls to the ground and dies, it remains only a single seed. But if it dies, it produces many seeds" (Jn 12:23-24).

For a seed in the ground, covered and warm, three days is good germination time. The miracle of Jesus' body, three days dead, brought to glorious new life, promises hope for all the degradations of creation.

This Lord of all longs to pull us and all of creation out of our degradation and into his life. The conjunction of Easter and spring in the northern hemisphere is neither chance nor early Christian syncretism. What happened in that garden nearly twenty centuries ago is the key to God's wish for his world.

Easter is therefore an entirely appropriate time to talk about gardens: the planting of the dead flower heads that we call seeds in the tomb we call soil; the resurrection of seedlings as they throw back soil and stone to burst from their grave in vigor and life; and the final harvest of those plants, "pleasing to the eye and good for food" (Gn 2:9).

Thus in the simple act of planting a seed, we dig deep down into the richness of life. As Christians we continually bump up against these "more thans"—the overflowing cups of God's goodness and love in all the days of our life. Sex is more than sensual pleasure; meals are more than human feeding times; communion is more than bread and wine. And the garden is more than planting and harvesting.

So in our own backyard, in garden or window box (or, for apartment dwellers, our own sunny window), we are in some small ways returning to the task set for Adam and Eve in the Garden of Eden. They were to tend the garden. Each of us in our own ways, with our particular insights and abilities, can take care of and protect some of the garden of God's whole creation. And may we, after a hard and sweaty day's work, know with joy that the wounded God still walks with us in his garden.

SOIL

"There's naught as nice as th' smell o' good clean earth, except th' smell o' fresh growin' things when th' rain falls on 'em."
—Frances Hodgson Burnett, *The Secret Garden*

Gardening begins and ends with the soil. From seed to compost, everything we put in the soil eventually affects much more than the plants we grow in it. Here are some suggestions for ways to care for the soil, to plant in such a way that we protect not only water systems and animal life, but the soil itself.

Since the advent of chemical fertilizers, our main way of replacing nutrients has been to dump on pellets and powders in whatever combination was appropriate for the time and crop. In most cases the stuff in itself is not particularly dangerous; it just bypasses the soil. So used alone, without the replacement of organic matter as soil enrichment, our gardens and fields can become lifeless growing mediums.

We are beginning to relearn an ancient lesson: the basic tending of the garden is the tending of the soil itself. And that means returning to the soil most of the materials we have taken from it. Good gardening—good agriculture—farms the soil first of all: good crops follow. This concern for returning organic matter to the soil is one of the most obvious ways in which we are nourished by cycles: in this case the cycle of growth, eating, waste, and decay into fertile soil. Here are some basic principles for "planting" the soil.

Use Natural Fertilizers. Compost and manure are the old reliable standbys. If you use fresh manure, dig it in at least one month before planting. For regular feeding, here are two inexpensive and effective fertilizers.

Teas. Put a shovelful of manure (fresh or dried), compost, garden weeds (nettles are especially good), or seaweed (dried and hosed-down or rained on) in a bucket; fill with water. Let the concoction sit for a few days (brewing times will vary) till the tea is good and strong: color and smell are good indicators. Fertilize with the tea. Transplants will take off especially well with manure or seaweed tea.

Fish fertilizers. Highly concentrated and very smelly, but one bottleful may last several seasons if you have a small garden. It needs to be mixed with water.

Rotate Crops. Be sure your beans and peas travel around the garden from year to year. They "plant" nitrogen in your soil. Rotation also keeps especially hungry crops like corn from depleting the same soil year after year. Certain soil-resident molds and fungi (in plants like tomatoes, cabbage, and broccoli) will be more likely to disappear if their host plant is moved.

Plant Cover Crops. (Also called "green mulch" or "green manure.") In the fall, when your garden season is almost over, till the plant material back into the ground and plant a good cover crop like rye grass, flax, corn salad, crimson clover, or buckwheat. Or better yet, as each part of the garden is harvested, till it and plant the cover crop. Cover crops keep the weeds down and, when turned under in the spring, add valuable nutrients.

Use Those Weeds. Some gardeners swear by their weeds and eat them along with their salad crops. But if you just want to do them in, choose a hot day not too long after a rain (they'll be easier to pull up by the roots) and lay them out between the plants and rows to dry. The roots will dry enough to keep them from settling back in, and the greenery will be a good mulch and quickly revert to soil. (You'll quickly discover exceptions; some weeds spread so perniciously that they shouldn't even be allowed in the compost pile.)

Mulch for Moisture and Weed Control. Straw, newspapers, grass clippings, and most leaves keep down weeds and keep in moisture. Some leaves, such as walnut leaves and eucalyptus, as well as evergreen needles, should be partly composted.

Mulches can harbor hungry bugs and slugs, however, so keep a margin free next to your plants. (*The Mulch Book*, by Stu Campbell, revised and updated by Donna Moore, Storey Publishing, 1991, gives much mulch advice.)

Compost. Discussed under "Yard Waste" in chapter three, good compost is gardener's gold. If you just don't want to face composting or have no place for a compost bin, try one of these shortcuts:

Compost stew: At the end of the day put green compost material into the blender and spin till you have a "stew." Use the stew to water house or garden plants. Egg shell "stew" provides not only nutrients but a decorative bed for your houseplants.

Bag-it compost: Put your compost in a sealed black plastic bag and let it sit in the sun, turning and shaking it every so often till you have a good black mess. This is fast, but "critters" may want a taste, so be careful.

Buried treasure compost: Collect your compost in a plastic container with a lid. When the container is full march out to your garden (or the shrubbery in front of your apartment) and bury your treasure. Empty the compost into a hole at least a foot deep to discourage the casual exhuming of your eggshells and orange peels by animals or gardeners, and pick a new spot each time. *Eventually* it will turn into soil.

Water Wisely. For water conservation as well as good root systems, timing and good watering equipment are important. Remember to mulch too: the best way to cut down on water usage.

—Water in the evening so the plants will be able to use the water before the sun has its turn.
—Water well when you do water. When you stick your finger in the soil, it should be moist all the way down.

—Watering times should be as far apart as possible, consistent with your crops' needs.

—Use a system that conserves water. Sprinkling systems water the air as well as the soil, which is usually an unacceptable waste.

Soaker hoses (with the tap turned low) can save up to seventy percent on water usage.

Drip irrigation or gravity flow can take some trouble to install, but over time it is the most economical system for water usage.

Controlling pests and problems—"naturally." Nothing makes it more obvious that there is something wrong in our relationship to creation than in the gardener's attitude toward "pests." Slugs, aphids, and cutworms are admirable creatures, undeniably a part of God's good creation. At the same time, no gardener feels very kindly toward them.

This is not the place to reflect on the nature of the cosmic tragedy that made these creatures terrors to us (and us terrors to them). What we can do (till we learn ways of coexisting with what we now call insect pests) is to use ways that are less poisonous to the whole web of creaturely life. Here are some poison-free solutions to problems caused by three garden terrors. For more, look in the garden guides listed at the end of this chapter.

Biergarten binge: Serve beer to slugs. Put the cheapest beer you can buy in a tuna can buried flush with the top of the soil. It will bring slugs in from the fields of sin for the last spree of their life. Empty the cans and the happily-drowned slugs the morning after.

Midnight raid: Cutthroats can go out well after dark with a flashlight and pick worms, slugs, and other bugs off their feast and drop them in a small container of salt water. Put the lid on after you're done. Wait a few days and dump them out. You must do this several nights in a row to be effective. Be sure to keep score; it adds spice to an otherwise unpleasant job.

Water wars and rotenone revenge: A hard spray of water will knock the aphids off your plants. A dusting of rotenone, a harmless plant product, will keep them from breathing.

VEGETABLES

Just the words "vegetable garden" bring to mind pictures of homey, wholesome country life—precisely what most of us don't have. Few have the space or the time for the traditional garden. We lose something, however, when we don't grow any of our own food: a sense of the cycles in which creation moves; the patterns of growth and decay in the seasons. We don't see the implications and the importance of all that happens to our food, from seed in the ground to beans in our mouth. And we cut ourselves off from conscious participation in God's way of sustaining us through his creation.

"I give you every seed-bearing plant on the face of the whole earth... for food" were God's words to Adam at the beginning. Adam *means* humanity, and these are God's words to us too. When we watch seeds grow into salad, we are seeing creation. At every meal God is saying to us: "I give you...."

We reply with a "thank you" which is usually superficial. But growing even a little of our own food can make that mealtime blessing a statement of substance rather than a rattled-off form. Here are three kinds of gardens: one of them, or a combination, should allow most people to grow at least some of what they eat.

In (and out) the Window. You don't have room for a garden? Start off with that Italian standby, a pot of basil in your kitchen window. Be sure to get seed of the compact bush variety, *ocimum basilicum minimum.* Use your bush for fresh, homegrown pesto for your pasta supper. From there you can branch out to parsley, sage, rosemary, and thyme—and even add lettuce and tomatoes for a salad. All will thrive indoors with a little care in pruning, watering, and light (though parsley will need a very deep pot for its long tap root). You can enjoy fresh herbs year-round.

If you have only a north window try mint, or supplement with a "gro-lite" fluorescent bulb that supplies full-spectrum light. Try transplanting nasturtium seedlings into water (with a little charcoal added to keep the water fresh) for a cascade of color and edible decor for your salad.

For help and ideas on this sort of gardening see *The Indoor Kitchen Garden: Vegetable Growing in Limited Space*, by Joy Spoczynska (San Francisco: Harper and Row, 1989).

On the Porch, Deck, or Balcony. Here, with fresh air and not that much care, you can grow a whole garden in containers. Be aware that your porch produce will probably need more frequent fertilizing. If you have a sunny porch or deck, you can start your spring with climbing peas. As they finish, plant pole beans; for beauty as well as nutrition, try scarlet runners. Root crops such as beets and carrots will need deep pots.

Grow cucumbers, squash, and even watermelons on a trellis. Beware, however, of assuming that bush varieties are your answer. They may take less handling, but they'll also produce less fruit. In the case of zucchini, of course, you may welcome this tendency—unless the midnight unloading of zucchini onto your neighbor's porch gives you satisfaction.

Or try a hanging salad. Get a wire basket and line it with moistened moss. Mix good-quality potting soil with some vermiculite or perlite (mineral material that helps soil retain water), and a quarter-cup of time-release vegetable fertilizer. Add this mixture a layer at a time, sticking lettuce seedlings through holes in the moss. Offset the plants in each layer and use a variety of leafy lettuces: buttercrunch, red-leaf, and so on. Mix some johnny-jump-ups and pansies for edible flower decor. Trailing nasturtiums in the bottom layer will hang down nicely. Some chives on the top layer will provide onion garnish and tasty flowers.

Keep well-watered and fertilized, and in a few weeks you'll have an easy-to-reach salad outside your door. Pick off the outer leaves, and the inner ones should keep coming.

Right on the Lawn. Edible landscaping is for those who cannot quite see themselves getting into the standard garden role but would like to have a lawn where more than the green grass grows. Aside from the vastness of the North American continent, what often awes people from other countries is the relatively vast expanse of private land surrounding the average suburban home. Rather than drugging this good land with downers of weedkiller and uppers of fertilizer and then spending every summer Sunday mowing, a more responsible use of our bit of God's creation might be to make it at least in part an edible fruit and vegetable garden.

Edible landscaping therefore is for those who would like to keep the "lawn" looking nice and have a garden too. Some vegetables are pretty enough to blend right into the flower garden: rhubarb chard, red-stem spinach, red romaine lettuce, russian kale, romanesco broccoli, the variegated leaves of apple mint and tri-color sage, the brilliant red flowers of pineapple sage, the dark rich wine of opal basil. All these belie our assumption that flowers are "pretty" and edible things are not. And of course, some beautiful flowers are highly edible: nasturtiums and pansies, for example. Fill in with a ground cover of corn salad, a lacey nook of carrots, and a background of scarlet runner beans and you'll have a beautifully and edibly landscaped "lawn."

Selecting Seeds. Someone observed that "all the flowers of tomorrow are in the seeds of today." That's not just a pretty truism. Much of creation's beauty and bounty is passed from generation to generation in these fragile containers, and we are in danger of forgetting that fact when we unquestioningly get our seeds from paper envelopes. Various things threaten the diversity and integrity of seed stocks; here are some ways you can exercise stewardship over seeds, an important means of caring for creation.

Buy untreated seeds. Many seeds come with various toxic treatments, which in most cases are unnecessary. Here are two excellent sources of untreated seeds. (Note that seeds—but not root stock and bulbs—can be shipped across the U.S./ Canadian border.)

—William Dam Seeds (Offer many Dutch varieties), P.O. Box 8400, Dundas, Ontario, Canada L9H 6M1.
—Seeds Blum, Idaho City Stage, Boise, ID 83706. Especially good for vegetable seeds.

Save your own seeds. Contact the Heritage Seed Program (address below) for the inexpensive, illustrated, and thorough HSP Seed-Saving booklet. Cost (including shipping) in 1991 is $5.50 Canadian—a real bargain. (If you live in the U.S., just send a check for $5.50 and consider the exchange loss a donation to a very worthy cause.)

Experiment with one older, nonhybrid, less well-known variety a year. If you are willing to save your own seeds from older, reliable varieties, you can take an active and important part in the increasingly urgent efforts to preserve seed diversity. The problem with hybrids is that most of them do not keep their high quality from generation to generation, but degenerate into inferior plants in successive generations. The two organizations listed below will put you in touch with seed sources and provide information on how to save seeds. And if by chance you are growing your grandfather's favorite tomatoes or a cherished family heirloom flower, these people would like to hear from you.

—Seed Saver's Exchange, R.R. 3, Box 329, Decorah, IA 52101.
—Heritage Seed Program, R.R. 3, Uxbridge, Ontario, Canada L0C 1K0.

Try some self-seeding vegetables. Many vegetables will self-sow naturally if left in a garden. A few rotten tomatoes left out over the winter may well start off on their own come spring. To harness this tendency, try such self-starters as corn salad and Russian kale.

Grow some of your own protein. Try soybeans, fava beans, or even wheat. A two-foot-by-five-foot patch should give you at least enough grain for a good hearty loaf of whole wheat bread. For ample help in the journey from seed to loaf, see *The Bread Book*, by Thom Leonard (Brookline, MA: East West Health Books, 1990).

For more information on seeds, edible landscaping, root charts, sun charts, *and* recipes, see *Designing and Maintaining Your Edible Landscape Naturally*, by Robert Kourik (Santa Rosa, CA: Metamorphic Press, 1986).

TREES

Trees are the largest living things in creation; some of them also, so far as we know, are the oldest. Among living things they are the most visible and the most spectacular. They are also among the most mysterious and awe-inspiring; perhaps because in their form they invite comparison with human beings. The man blind from birth saw "men like trees walking," though he had seen neither men nor trees before. Perhaps he was reflecting the observation in Psalm 1:3 that the righteous man is "like a tree planted by streams of water, which yields its fruit in season and whose leaf does not wither."

Some Tree Facts
—Through photosynthesis, trees release oxygen into the air: forests have been called the "lungs of the planet."
—Trees remove carbon dioxide, the major cause of global warming from the atmosphere, an average tree fixing about twenty-six pounds every year.

—Trees release significant amounts of moisture into the air. This process is hard to measure, but evident through the rainfall decline in deforested areas.

—Both through shade and the cooling produced through evaporation, trees can reduce the demand for air-conditioning by at least half.

—Some trees produce fruit and nuts, significantly contributing to food supplies not only for people but for birds and animals.

—Trees are still the major cooking fuel for over half the world's people.

—Trees are the source of wood for building and fiber for paper.

Both living and dead, trees have always been an important part of human life. Not only eating their fruit but resting in their shade has been with us from the beginning. Deforestation is nothing new either: both the Mediterranean area and much of China, for example, were once heavily forested.

What is unique in our own time is the destruction of so much forest in a relatively short time, largely to feed our demand for wood products and for open land. Much of this deforestation goes on in the tropics, but not all. By many measures the greatest forest of all (nearly twice as productive as the tropical rain forest in sheer weight of living material) is the temperate rain forest that once reached unbroken along the Pacific coast from California to Alaska. In our lifetime most of it has been destroyed—replaced, if at all, by tree farms of incomparably less richness and diversity.

What can you do? One thing is to plant a tree. Planting one-hundred million trees in the cities would reduce carbon dioxide emission in the U.S. by eighteen million tons and (through the indirect benefit of cooling) reduce energy consumption by forty billion kilowatt hours.

Some Cautions. Not all tree planting is good, however; here are a few reservations:[1]

1. In some places trees should *not* be planted. God didn't cover the whole planet with trees, and it can be as much a desecration to try to plant a forest in a desert as to turn a forest into a desert.
2. The wrong tree in the right place can be a problem. You must plant a tree native to the place, which will fit into the life of that place. Some tree-planting programs have been disasters for native plant and animal life.
3. Planting of baby forests is often promoted by the same groups eager to cut down (and profit from) old forests. So make sure your tree planting is coupled with opposition to the destruction of remaining old-growth forests (see below).

But Do Plant!

—Plant trees by your home for shading, beauty, and food. Some research might be needed to determine the best kind. But planting a tree is very simple. If a large tree, as tall as a person, it may cost a few dollars from a nursery, but it will begin almost immediately to give pleasure and to do its work in caring for creation in your own backyard. Fruit trees will begin to bear significantly in a few years.

—Plant for the future. Some nut trees will not bear significantly for a decade or two, and some trees will not mature till after you are dead. But don't plant just for yourselves: plant for the next generation.

—Plant trees around churches. Churches, which often are surrounded by quite a bit of area, can be good places to plant trees—not just ornamental trees, either, but trees of whatever species grow in the area. Churches ought to be "creation awareness centers," and planting trees is one of the best ways to begin.

Preserve Trees

Oppose the cutting of old forests. You can also work to stop the logging of the last remnants of old forests. Forests are far more than trees; they are complex communities of living things. In these forests the role of a dead tree—which may lie rotting for half a millennium—is as important as the role of a live one. The argument sometimes advanced that it's necessary to harvest "over-mature" timber is fallacious. (How did the old-growth forest get to be so healthy—and so desirable for lumber—in the first place?)

These objections to the logging of the last old-growth forests are not an opposition to logging itself: tree farming is an appropriate practice, though still in its infancy. What is essential is to preserve the pockets of forest ecosystems that we still have.

For an aesthetically and scientifically superb introduction to the mystery of North America's rain forest, read David Kelly and Gary Braasch, *Secrets of the Old-Growth Forest* (Salt Lake City: Peregrine Smith Books, 1990).

Leave trees on building lots. The construction industry, for obvious reasons, would like to be able to build on a bare lot. It costs more to save the trees. But whenever possible we need to ask architects and builders to work around existing trees, rather than leveling the lot and "re-landscaping" it afterward—often with smaller, alien, decorative species.

This is especially true of our church construction projects. Good things are seen by a community when people who know the Creator take some extra time and money to preserve creation where they worship the Lord. For as the psalmist says, it ultimately is the Lord who plants and waters the trees.

FLOWERS

In the doldrums of winter, one by one the seed catalogues start arriving. Any sensible person will send off promptly for reliable vegetable seeds. But many of us end up purchasing those practical seeds at the corner store seed rack, having whiled away our winter evenings in a world of yellow daffodils, blue cornflowers, and orange and red poppies. We dream of back borders, rock gardens, hanging baskets, and window boxes. We're reduced to mere marveling by the effort of choosing among the wild extravaganza of color and form in dahlias, gladiolis, irises, and tulips.

Flowers are not humanly useful, in the same practical way as are trees, vegetables, and herbs. But though we can't build houses with them, they make a home; though we don't usually eat them, our hearts and eyes feast on them; and though most have no medicinal value, we take them to sick people.

Through their role in plant reproduction, flowers play an important role in the development and sustaining of creation. But the sheer exuberance and diversity of flowers speak of more than the ecological value of diversity or success in attracting a pollinator for the survival of the species. Flowers declare most clearly that their reason for being is joy. They sit by the altars of our churches and shout the glory of God through many a dull sermon. Like all the infinite variety of the created world, flowers are God's way of saying "I am."

Revel in Seed Catalogues. Looking through these seed catalogues is almost as good as growing the flowers. Keep a stack by your bed for a good night-time browse, and you'll fall asleep with visions of sweet peas in your dreams. Sometimes the transition to actually ordering and planting flowers is difficult, but the pictures are still helping you glory in God's creation and perhaps reminding you of the paradise to come.

One way to cope with the rather alarming inertia you may discover when the moment finally comes to order some seeds is to decide what you enjoy most about flowers and go for that. Here are some flowers matched to some particular joys.

A Fragrance Garden. Mignonette (not startlingly beautiful, but a wonderful smell), allysum, evening-scented stocks (planted with virginia stocks), stocks (ten-week stocks grow quickly and last long), sweet peas (especially the older varieties), scented geraniums, narcissus, hyacinths, lilacs, sweet violets, lily of the valley, honeysuckle, and (of course) roses. See: *The Fragrant Year: Scented Plants for Your Garden and Your House,* by Helen Van Pelt Wilson and Leonie Bell (New York: William Morrow, 1967).

A Butterfly Garden. Butterflies not only wing in color and life to your garden; they pollinate your flowers, their larval stages provide food for birds; and they are good evidence of the health of creation. Some butterfly-catchers are lavender, thyme, cosmos, nicotiana, purple coneflower, allysum, lychnis, daisies, garden phlox, butterfly bush, sweet rocket, tagetes marigold, and stinging nettles. Butterflies need water too, so keep a mud puddle or wet spot available. See *Butterfly Gardening: Creating Summer Magic in Your Garden* by Xerces Society, Smithsonian Institute, Whitecap Books (Canada). Published in the U.S. by Sierra Club Books and National Wildlife Federation, 1990.

A Bird Garden. Again, as for butterflies, a puddle or shallow fresh water birdbath is an important part of a bird garden. Good flowers are zinnias, cosmos, tithonia, sunflowers, beebalm monardas, foxglove, and snapdragons. See the booklet *A Gardener's Guide to Birds,* Rodale Press, 33 E. Minor St., Emmaus, PA 18098.

An Evening Garden. White or light-colored flowers belong in a garden to be walked through at dusk. The scent of many flowers is strongest at this time of day. Try white allysum, evening stocks, sweet rocket, nicotiana, sweet peas, honeysuckle, and superb pink. Look for the white or pale stronglyscented varieties.

A Wild Garden. The plants will vary in every area, and you will do the ecosystem of your area a great favor by planting *locals*—or what used to be locals for your particular area.

Much damage has been done by homesick people who import their favorite wild plants, which then proceed to squeeze out the natives.

Find a nursery or garden club near you and ply them with questions. Take a flower identification book into nearby natural areas and find out what's there. Keep track of your favorites and gather a few seeds later—or order from Wildseed (P.O. Box 308, Eagle Lake, TX 77434), *if* the variety is the same. Propagation of wildflower seeds is often difficult. For advice, write to the National Wildlife Research Center (2600 FM 973 North, Austin, TX 78725-4201). They can tell you which flowers *should* be growing in your area and give you advice on growing them.

A Dry Garden. "Xeriscaping"—landscaping with drought-resistant plants is a good idea in water-shortage areas (see chapter one section on water use). Some desert plants are both spectacular and rare, but be sure they are appropriate for your area. Other plants that flourish with little water are lupines, iris, poppies, black-eyed susans, sea holly, garden pinks, portulaca rock roses, lychnis (coronaria), and cosmos.

A Garden of Beautiful Names. Most of these flowers have earned their name through long familiarity due to the ease and grace with which they settle in almost anywhere: meadow-sweet, johnny jump-ups (also called heart's ease, love-in-idleness and herb trinity), love-lies-bleeding, sea holly, foxglove, Jacob's ladder, snowdrops, lady's mantle (or lady's coat), love in a mist (also called devil in a bush). And finally, three campanulas: bell-flower, fairy's thimble, and bats in the belfry. Collect the names, if not the flowers. For more names (and the seeds) write Chiltern Seeds, Bortree Stile, Ulverston, Cumbria LA127PB, England.

For cutting flowers, check in garden shops for these inexpensive shears: the *Gardenia* flower-gatherer. This is four tools in one: a blade to give the stem a clean cut, a spring clip to hold the cut bloom, a thorn-stripping notch for roses, and a serrated stem-crusher to increase water absorption.

GOOD GARDEN GUIDES

For General Advice: Rodale Books Incorporated has a wonderfully enticing collection of helpful books. Here are two new books with interesting formats and helpful advice. Both are geared to busy people who need basic information. Charts, tables, and lists make the information extremely accessible. Both books provide a good list of other reference material: books dealing with specific problems, tool sources, and seed catalogues. *The Weekend Garden Guide: Work-Saving Ways to a Beautiful Backyard* by Susan A. Roth (Emmaus, PA: Rodale Press, 1991). *Rodale's Illustrated Encyclopedia of Landscaping and Gardening Techniques,* edited by Barbara W. Ellis (Emmaus, PA: Rodale Press, 1990).

For more help go to your local nursery and find out what the nursery "bible" for your region is. Most areas have books geared to their particular gardening conditions and problems.

For the Sheer Glory of Gardens

In and Out of the Garden, by Sara Middan (New York: Workman Publishing, 1981). A work of art, full of garden tips and planting lore, woven in and around pictures, a true mesh of medium and message. Even the paperback version comes with a ribbon page marker.

Green Thoughts: A Writer in the Garden, by Eleanor Perenyi (New York: Vintage Books, 1981). Combines fine detail on specific subjects with excellent garden philosophizing. A few chapter headings hint at the diversity: "Frost," "Failures," "Paths," "Poppies," and a concluding chapter on the history of women in gardening, "Woman's Place."

Green Grows the Garden, by Margery Williams Bianco (New York: Macmillan, 1936). The author of *The Velveteen Rabbit* gives us a winsome and witty primer on gardening, for children and adults. This book is old. Look for it in secondhand shops; it's well worth the search.

The Flora: An Anthology of Poetry and Prose, compiled by Fiona MacMath (Oxford: Lion Publishing, 1990). This is no mere nosegay, but a wide and wonderful gathering from the deeply-rooted garden of words. The selections are organized topically and include a surprising little collection called "Lord Jesus Hath a Garden."

> *"... the world is God's walled garden..."*
> —Fiona MacMath

> *Then suddenly she saw her garden and the pain was gone. She leaned out the window, smelling the fresh scent of it, seeing how the colors glowed in the sunset. "I live to the full," she told herself. "All gardeners do."*
>
> —Margaret, in Elizabeth Goudge, *The Bird in the Tree*

❀ EIGHT ❀

Eating

Our home ground remains what it always has been: bloody ground and holy ground at once.
—Robert Farrar Capon, *The Third Peacock*

ECOLOGY HAS BEEN DESCRIBED AS the science of who is eating whom: and eating involves us unavoidably, continually, in creation's cycles of exchange. This is so upsetting to some that they abhor eating or turn to vegetarianism. There are, as we shall see, many good reasons for a vegetarian or near-vegetarian diet, but trying to escape the necessity of nourishing your life through other life is probably not one of them. Robert Farrar Capon puts it well: "Even a vegetarian creation is not the answer. It is only our human chauvinism that is satisfied when literal bloodshed is ruled out... the lettuces still, in their own way, take a dim view of having to cease being lettuces; as they can, they fight it...."[1]

All of this is to remind us—as the Lord's Supper does, and as every meal ought to—that eating, like life itself, is solemn and important business. It can be a celebration of creation—but it can also produce a great degradation of creation. In the following pages we suggest some ways we can make our eating more careful of the creation that sustains us.

SEARCH FOR THE SOURCES OF YOUR FOOD

We know what we like to eat, and we like to get it as cheaply and conveniently as possible. But the costs to creation of that convenience are often extreme. We've considered one of those costs already on the throwaway end: the packaging that keeps our food fresh and makes it marketable. But the most extreme costs to creation lie in the sources of our food.

There are two aspects to source: the *where* and the *how.*

Where Does My Food Come From? When buying fruits, vegetables, and other produce, ask the grocer where they come from. (In general, the larger the store the more trouble you'll have finding this out.) If there's a choice, buy foods grown close to home. Not only will they be fresher, but the considerable expense of transporting (usually under refrigeration) will be avoided. One study showed that the average food item had been transported an average of eight-hundred miles.

Often there will not be a choice—few of us have local access to bananas, coffee, or pineapple. Here the issue gets complicated. Many of our imported foods (coffee, tea, sugar, and bananas, for example) come from poorer countries in the south where workers are often exploited by a few wealthy landowners, and where cash-crop agriculture (for export) has monopolized the best land, sending subsistence farmers to steep, poor soils, further contributing to land degradation. (Sometimes the produce grown close to home is harvested by exploitative labor as well.)

One choice is simply to boycott materials grown under those conditions—but usually this is a simplistic and unsatisfactory solution, since the imported crop represents at least some income (meager as it is) to the people who produce it. Such boycotts are only effective if they are accompanied by vigorous political action as well. A better solution is to buy items which are not only grown, but processed in the home country. But we have few guarantees that even a small fraction of the dollar we pay for coffee here will go to a worker there (a notable exception is "Bridgehead" coffee). There is no easy solution: but the first step is knowing the source of the food.

How Is My Food Produced? Even more difficult questions are raised by asking *how* our food is produced. The sad fact is that in order to make animal protein available to us in high quality and at low price, we have increasingly turned farms into factories and animals into protein-producing machines. Many modern farms bear little resemblance to the idyllic image that most of us carry in our heads. An important book—well-researched and written with both passion and compassion—is John Robbins' *Diet for a New America* (Walpole, NH: Stillpoint Press, 1987). The book is frequently compared to Rachel Carson's *Silent Spring,* which thirty years ago alerted people to the danger of indiscriminate pesticide use. Robbins makes a strong case that our current farming methods are extremely cruel to animals and that these methods are driven by our consumption of far more protein than we need.

Eggs, for example, (the highest in cholesterol of all foods) are produced by chickens in extremely crowded conditions. Much of the egg needs for Los Angeles are provided by one "farm" that produces 2,200,000 eggs daily from three million hens.[2] These hens are housed five each in sixteen-by-eighteen-inch wire mesh cages, designed so waste automatically goes in one place and eggs in another. In such conditions a form of insanity causes chickens to peck each other, often to death—so they are debeaked. Another problem is that the toes of chickens grow around the wire mesh so they can't move. The solution: remove one of the toes before the chicken is put in the cage. The attitude behind such behavior is well-expressed in a farming journal (*Farmer and Stockbreeder*):

The modern layer is, after all, only a very efficient converting machine, changing the raw material—feedstuffs—into the finished product—the egg—less, of course, maintenance requirements.[3]

The same extreme crowding is typical of almost all large protein-producing farms. Cattle feedlots are a particularly unpleasant example. One university study recommended that the space per steer be fourteen square feet: the equivalent of thirteen one-thousand pound animals in a twelve-by-fifteen-foot room. Pigs, perhaps the most intelligent of farm animals, are reared in equally crowded conditions. They often grow from birth to butchering without ever seeing the light of day. Again, the attitude producers take is that they are forced by our food choices to regard the animals as food-producing machines, not as creatures with feelings. Consider these words from the journal *Hog Farm Management*: "Forget the pig is an animal. Treat him just like a machine in a factory. Schedule treatments like you would lubrication. Breeding season like the first step in an assembly line. And marketing like the delivery of finished goods."[4]

The Problem of Animal Sewage. Finally, we need to recognize the tremendous sewage problem raised by our livestock production. Livestock in the U.S. (according to John Robbins) produce twenty times as much excrement as the entire human population of the country. Even that would not be an intolerable load if it were distributed among small farms, but most of it is concentrated in enormous feedlots. The president of a large cattle company observed that "With 20,000 animals in our pens, we have a problem equal to a city of 320,000 people."[5]

Most of us are horrified when we learn these facts behind our daily food, and we should be. We Christians especially, who regard chickens, pigs, and cattle as fellow-creatures, have good reason to ask if this is the right kind of stewardship. The shape of that stewardship—and God's attitude when it is violated—is expressed by Ezekiel, who uses good and bad husbandry as a way of criticizing the leaders of Israel:

This is what the Sovereign Lord says:... Should not shepherds take care of the flock? You eat the curds, clothe yourselves with the wool and slaughter the choice animals, but you do not take care of the flock. You have not strengthened the weak or healed the sick or bound up the injured. You have not brought back the strays or searched for the lost. You have ruled them harshly and brutally.

—Ezekiel 34:2-4

Searching out the source of our food should lead us to buy milk, meat, and eggs very cautiously. And it may lead us as well to draw more carefully on the life of other creatures.

SAVE ENERGY IN EATING

To produce one pound of beef, we need sixteen pounds of grain and soybeans, 2500 gallons of water, and the energy equivalent of one gallon of gasoline.
—*50 Things You Can Do to Save the Planet*

Food is energy: it is the "fuel" on which our bodies run. Yet much of our food takes far more energy to grow, transport, and package than it provides to us. And as we have seen, our demands for energy are getting to be an increasingly harsh burden on creation itself. For that reason we need to consider not just the energy we get out of food but the energy that went into producing it. When we do, we see that a great deal is wasted—by packaging and processing, but more than anything else, by our insistence on eating high-meat meals.

When we eat meat we are eating "high on the food chain." That is, the animals we eat have eaten grains that we could ourselves eat. We have squandered (in the case of beef) about ninety percent of the food value. Thus ten times as many people can be supported on a vegetarian diet as a beef diet.

Vast amounts of energy would be saved by reducing our

meat intake: and the freed-up agricultural energy, water, and land could produce food more efficiently. One researcher has concluded that "over a billion people could be fed by the grain and soybeans eaten by U.S. livestock every year," and that "If Americans reduced their meat intake by just ten percent, the savings in grains and soybeans could adequately feed sixty million people—the number of peole who starve to death, worldwide each year."[6]

Americans eat fifty percent more protein on the average than the Recommended Daily Allowance; young children eat three times as much as they need. Excess protein in older people almost certainly contributes to osteoporosis. For most North Americans the problem is not getting enough protein—it is in having too *much* protein.

Here are some suggestions for saving energy in food:

Buy grass-fed beef. Cattle fed on pasture instead of fattened on grains produce protein twice as efficiently.

Switch to poultry, lamb, or fish. Turkey and chicken are more efficient ways of turning vegetable protein into meat protein than are pork and beef. But even chicken, the most efficient, wastes about five times what it produces.

Use meat for flavor. A little bacon or a pork hock can add lots of pork flavor without much pork. One steak or one chicken breast, sliced thin and stir-fried with vegetables, gives plenty of protein for a family of four. It's cheap, fast, and simple. And though it calls for more creativity in cooking, it does not necessarily require more time.

Eat Low on the Food Chain. Instead of eating the cow that ate the grain that used the water that watered the field where the grass used to grow—we can learn to eat the grains themselves. We have been led to believe that meals without meat (and milk, cheese, and eggs) are fattening, bland and boring, hard to make, insufficient for athletes and active people, or that they require careful planning to achieve balance of

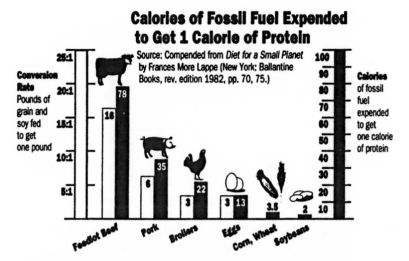

Calories of Fossil Fuel Expended to Get 1 Calorie of Protein

Source: Compended from *Diet for a Small Planet* by Frances More Lappe (New York: Ballantine Books, rev. edition 1982, pp. 70, 75.)

complementary proteins. All these points are false. Here are some suggestions for meatless alternatives.

—Use nut and seed butters and tofu in place of some uses of cheese and eggs.

—Eat more rice, beans, and potatoes (see the suggestion for a potato meal below).

—Learn to put grains, seeds, nuts, and legumes on center stage in a meal rather than in the wings as a side dish. Rice and beans are good dietary staples, supplying protein and fiber.

—Eat more bread. "Give us this day our daily bread" is not far off the mark as far as nutrition goes.

Potato Meal. Once a week have a Potato Night. Bake an oven-full of potatoes (preferably from a reliable, pesticide-free source). To make the skins soft and tasty, rub them very lightly with margarine before baking. In the center of the table put these potato toppings—or others you'd like. Use as many or as few as you like:

Chopped green onions or leeks
Chopped olives (black are best)
Chopped parsley
Crumbled tofu, fried in oil with a little soy sauce
Sliced, fried mushrooms
Grated cheese
Bits of bacon
Sour Cream
Butter
(These last four are not needed for protein but are for flavor.)

A "Lazy Susan" is very handy for this meal. Kids can be won over with the fun of choosing toppings. With a salad and fruit for dessert, baked potatoes become a good company meal. And all the leftover potatoes can be used for hashbrowns or potato salad.

For more information on meatless meals, see *Diet for a Small Planet* (be sure to get the revised edition) by Francis Moore Lappe (New York: Ballantine Books, 1982).

Potato farmers can regale you with tales of the superiority of potatoes as a food. One told us of a Texas prison experiment in which a small group of inmates volunteered to eat no meat, just variations on potatoes, for a whole year. All their fellow inmates got the standard meat menu, and guess who was healthier at the end of the year!

SUPPORT LOCAL GROWERS

One of the best things we can do to care for creation is to support local farmers who grow food in ways that do not degrade land, water, or the animals themselves. This means

To make a sustainable city, one must begin somehow, and I think the beginning must be small and economic. A beginning could be made, for example, by increasing the amount of food bought from farmers in the local countryside by consumers in the city. As the food economy becomes more local, local farming would become more diverse; the farms would become smaller, more complex in structure, more productive; and some city people would be needed to work on the farms. Sooner or later, as a means of reducing expenses both ways, organic wastes from the city would go out to fertilize the farms of the supporting region; thus city people would have to assume an agricultural responsibility....

—Wendell Berry, "Out of Your Car, Off Your Horse: Twenty-seven propositions about global thinking and the sustainability of cities." *The Atlantic Monthly*, February 1991, 63.

that we need to change our expectations of food simply *being there* in the supermarket when we want it, as though it had come off some food-producing assembly line. Farms should not be simply "food factories," however much the pressures of our time have pushed them in that direction. They rather should be places where old-fashioned words like *husbandry* and *stewardship* gain their meaning: places where human beings show their mastery not through cruelty or oppression but through kindness, care, and understanding.

The ideal of agriculture as *serving* the land is an ancient one: when Adam's task to till the garden is described in Genesis, the Hebrew word *abad* is used, a word that also means *serve.*

The massive shift of the last century, in which the population has gone from eighty percent rural to eighty percent urban, has left those of us in the cities rootless, with no knowledge of the earth and how it sustains us. As Wendell Berry puts it, "Our model citizen is a sophisticate who before puberty understands how to produce a baby, but who at the age of thirty will not know how to produce a potato."[7]

This shift has done as much damage to those who remain behind on the farm. It has either made farmers into a quaint relic from a bygone era, or it has forced them to be ultra-efficient businessmen for whom ideas of husbandry get in the way of success. The words of a modern cattle auctioneer are all too typical. When asked about the misery of the animals he disposed of, he replied:

> It doesn't bother me. We're no different from any other business. These animal rights people like to accuse us of mistreating our stock, but we believe we can be most efficient by not being emotional. We are a business, not a humane society, and our job is to sell merchandise at a profit. It's no different from selling paper clips, or refrigerators.[8]

Such an attitude does not at all reflect care or stewardship for the animals themselves. To treat animals as nothing more than raw material or merchandise is to deny a part of our very humanity. It's clear then that an important task is to begin to reunite culture and agriculture: to require that the food we eat be produced not only cheaply and efficiently but humanely. And one way of doing that is to support local farms and farmers.

Obviously our ability to do this will vary a great deal from place to place. Yet even in the middle of a big city, we can find grocers who make an attempt to buy locally. Often such grocers are not in the large supermarket chains, which have contracts requiring them to buy everything from one supplier. A friend of ours in Washington state tried to get the local store of a large supermarket chain to buy the produce of local cherry orchards, but found that the chain had a contract with a supplier in Michigan. Further investigation revealed that most of the cherries sold locally ended up being shipped to Michigan! Here are some ways of avoiding this kind of absurdity:

Find Stores that Carry Local Produce Wisely Grown. Organic or natural food stores are often a good source. Sometimes labels help: a group called FACT (Farm Animals Concern Trust) lets their trademark (NEST EGGS) be used by farms meeting their standard.

Be Willing to Pay More. Meat, eggs, vegetables, and milk produced with methods that are kind to soil and animals will cost more.

Support Farmer's Markets. These markets carry on an ancient tradition in which farmers on certain days bring their produce into town. Beware, though: some who sell at these get their produce at the same mass suppliers as the food stores.

Visit Nearby Farms. Find farmers who will sell produce directly, or allow you to pick it yourself.

Above all, get to know the people who produce your food and learn from them. Where possible, become a kind of "farmer" yourself, in your own backyard or window box. (See "Protect Farms" in the next chapter.)

SERVE GOOD FOOD

When an archaeologist recently turned his attention from excavating Mayan ruins to excavating our landfills, he discovered many fascinating things. He found, for example, that the largest part of our garbage is paper, and that buried papers were often still legible after fifteen years. But what he found even more surprising was the number of hotdogs—as old as the newspapers and perfectly preserved. Obviously the preservatives were doing their work, perhaps too well. The embalmed hot dogs are a grim reminder of the kind of things we regularly eat—and an inspiration to eat better food. Here are some general guidelines for eating.

Read the Label: Labels are required by law to show what additives are in your food. They usually do that pretty accurately. You need to get in the habit of reading the labels and knowing your additives. Additives are used for color, flavor, preservation, and texture, and are certainly not all bad. Many common additives are made from harmless natural substances. Carotene, rennet, pectin, lecithin, agar, and tartaric acid all come from natural sources, ranging from calf stomachs to seaweed and all are quite harmless. Even ominous-sounding additives like mono- and di-glycerides, calcium propionate, and ascorbic acid (another name for Vitamin C) are naturally produced substances and are fine to eat.

Other additives, especially recently-synthesized chemicals, are not so innocent. Though they may have proven harmless in small doses, there's no good way to test for cumulative effects. Increasing allergies, sterility, and even hyperactivity in young children have been tentatively linked to minute amounts of food additives. Until the results of testing over a whole lifespan are available, we should be suspicious of synthesized additives. Additives that have shown some tendency to produce cancer include artificial sweeteners and colorings, BHA, BHT, and nitrite and nitrate preservatives.

Not all additives are labeled. Many have not been deliberately added, but are unwanted leftovers: residues from things added during growth or production. Labels do *not* include information on the following substances, which many consider to be very dangerous:

—Pesticides: residues in food from sprays and contaminated ground water.
—Antibiotics; growth hormones in animals; growth regulators in plants.
—Preservative wax coating on fruits and vegetables.
—Cleaning or preserving fungicides.

Avoid Substitutes. Cream in your coffee or whipped cream may be bad for you, but a chemical substitute is not necessarily better. Read with suspicion the long list of ingredients that go to make up chemical concoctions like artificial topping or coffee "whitener."

Avoid Processed Foods. Buy fresh fruits and vegetables. If you do buy processed foods, compare labels. When buying processed meats, for example, check with the butcher to see if there is an "in-house" counter variety that is without preservatives.

Question the Outward Appearance. If the surface is shiny, richly colored, super-clean, or unblemished, ask yourself why. Each of those traits may be due *not* to its being wholesome, healthy, farm-fresh produce but to chemical fix-its.

Grow Some of Your Own. Anyone can grow lettuce, tomatoes, and beans—and by doing so you can ensure that those vegetables will be relatively free of additives.

Eat Seasonally. Although there is no doubting the good of lettuce and oranges in the middle of a January blizzard, we have carried to an extreme our having to have any food when and where we want it. One of the reasons that the average food item travels so far before it gets on our table is that we ignore the limits imposed on our appetite by creation itself. It is a good discipline to adjust our eating habits to what is seasonally available from local growers. The effort will make us more aware of the cycle of the seasons and more appreciative of things when they are in season.

Eat In, Not Out. Save eating out for special occasions, and then go to restaurants that make an effort to get their food from good sources. We can't read the labels when we eat at a restaurant, and many restaurants use their own chemicals to preserve freshness.

Cook Your Own Food. Rather than relying on packaged, pre-pared foods, spend a family day once a month concocting soups and stews of the sort that made Esau give up his birthright. Then freeze the concoctions in meal-sized portions. One doctor/mother we know cooks up the best chili we've ever tasted and freezes meal-sized portions for her office nights. Or when you do make a soup, stew, or casserole double the amount and save the intentional leftovers for next week. Soups and stews improve with age.

Get Some Good Cookbooks. *The Moosewood Cookbook,* by Mollie Katzen, and *Sundays at The Moosewood Restaurant,* quickly put to rest the fears that meatless meals take hours to prepare and taste bland. You may wish to reduce the fat and salt content of the recipes. For example, use half the oil called for, and substitute yogurt for cream. *The New Laurel's Kitchen* by Laurel Robertson, Carol Flinders, and Brian Ruppenthal is packed with up-to-date nutritional information. *More-with-Less Cookbook,* provided by the Mennonite Central Committee, is a classic of good, low-energy eating (and doesn't exclude chocolate chips). *From a Monastery Garden* by Victor-Antoine d'Avila-Latourrette is a cookbook to feed your mind and soul as well as your body. It includes a superb preface by Elise Boulding and scattered quotes from people as diverse as Augustine, Charles Dickens, and Rose Kennedy.

Score Your Eating Habits! *Nutrition Scoreboard* is a bright poster that rates foods with a score of 1 to 100, based on nutritional value including such factors as additives, sugar, and fat content. Hang it up on the wall or fridge and let the kids keep score. This is available from Center for Science in the Public Interest, 1875 Connecticut Avenue NW, Suite 300, Washington, DC 20009-5728, or call 202-667-7483.

NINE

Protecting

... all worthy things that are in peril as the world now stands, those are my care. And for my part, I shall not wholly fail of my task, though Gondor should perish, if anything passes through this night that can still grow fair or bear fruit and flower again in days to come. For I also am a steward.

—J.R.R. Tolkien, *The Return of the King*

I N GENESIS ADAM IS TOLD TO "have dominion" or to "rule" over every creature on earth. Many have understood that command to be disastrous for the health of the planet: and indeed we all have seen the damage done by a thoughtless, self-serving notion of human superiority. But a closer look at biblical dominion shows us that it is most clearly seen in Jesus: most clearly seen, in fact, in the cross. Fundamentally, God's dominion over us is costly to God; it is protective; it is saving. So our dominion over creation should also be a saving and protecting one *and* may well be costly.

This caring dominion is also implied in Genesis. Adam is placed in the garden to "till" it. (We have already seen how the root meaning of that word is "serve.") But he is also to keep, to watch, to preserve—in short, to protect. The same word is used a little later in Genesis when Cain asks, "Am I my brother's keeper?" The answer to his question is clearly yes;

and if our Creator asks of us, "Are you creation's keeper?" The answer should clearly be the same. Whether we keep it poorly or well, we can't shrug off the mantle of "earthkeeper."

We speak in this chapter of four things we ought to cherish and protect: water and habitat, both in quantity and quality; the farm, which keeps people in a sustainable relationship with creation; and the family, that human institution within which all our patterns of care are formed and nurtured.

PROTECT HABITAT

> *Woe to you who add house to house*
> *and join field to field*
> *till no space is left*
> *and you live alone in the land.* —Isaiah 5:8

One of the intriguing things about Psalm 104 (it has been called the "ecologist's psalm," and we have quoted it before in this book) is its deep sense not only that God is Creator of all but that he makes *places* for each creature. The birds of the air nest by the waters; grass grows for the cattle; the stork has its home in the pine trees; the high mountains belong to the wild goats; the crags are a refuge for the coney.

Till recently, most men and women have lived with a clear sense of their proximity to other creatures, even those they do not use. The value of all creatures is reflected in the Noah story, where livestock, useful to humanity, is mentioned *after* "every wild animal." Thus the divine concern is primarily for all creatures, not just those useful to humanity.

We are steadily reducing the places for such creatures for whom we have no obvious use. This is probably bad for us (in the long run). But as stewards of the Creator, preserving our own well-being is not our main motive anyway. Our purpose is to serve and enjoy God, which involves caring for and enjoying his creation.

There are many things we can do to make space for other creatures. We are not at this point going to consider the problem of massive habitat destruction in large wild areas like the rain forest, but will look closer to home.

Learn what plants and animals are native to your place. (We talk more about ways and reasons for doing that in chapter ten, in the section "Name Creation.")

Be willing to let your house, office, church, or farm be surrounded by native vegetation. Sometimes we are too concerned with neatness and efficiency. If we can't *use* every square foot of space under our care, we assume that it at least needs to be landscaped or planted as lawn. Leave areas in natural vegetation where possible. That will provide habitat for native plants and animals.

Often this "leaving" requires quite a bit of activity. In our area, for example, native vegetation is often overwhelmed by the voracious, fast-growing Scotch broom plant (which, legend has it, was introduced by a homesick Scottish clergyman). The only way to protect native vegetation is to energetically uproot and burn the broom plants, taking care to disturb other vegetation as little as possible.

Leave and protect little wild areas. As farms and fields have grown in size, fencerows (and in England, hedgerows) are steadily being eliminated. Yet these small strips of untilled ground, sometimes only a foot or two wide, can be enormously valuable as habitat for native plants, birds, and small mammals. Since the area is not tilled from year to year, it provides protection for nests, burrows, and forage. (Railroad, power-line, and highway right-of-ways are often—ironically—similar havens for native wild things.)

Reintroduce—or attract—native plants and animals. Often, especially in urban areas, it is too late to preserve anything of original wildlife. But we can, perhaps, with some study and care, bring that life back. (See "Re-Member Creation," in chapter ten.)

Birds are a good place to begin. Feeding stations allow bird populations to thrive even in the city. In cold climates, heated birdbaths can provide a crucial supply of water. Carefully designed nest-boxes can be used to reintroduce birds to an area where their original habitat was destroyed. Contact your local Audubon society for particular advice on providing habitat for birds in your area.

Learn to be a swamp-lover. Wetlands are not only the most productive of wildlife habitats, they also are the most threatened. The same shallow marshland that provides a home to so many birds, plants, and animals is easily drained, filled, and converted to cheap land for shopping malls, airports, and housing developments. The quiet richness and beauty of these places often goes undefended. And Christians ought to be defenders of the defenseless, human or not.

PROTECT WATER

> *All praise be yours, my Lord, through Sister Water,*
> *So useful, lowly, precious, and pure.*
> —St. Francis, "Canticle of the Sun"

We have already considered the need to reduce our wasting of water, but there is another problem, in some ways more serious: we have to be concerned with the *quality* of water, even in the vast oceans. It's good to start at home. Where does your water come from? What watershed do you live in? (Some have argued that watersheds are a much wiser way to divide the land than the rather arbitrary divisions of state, province, and county.) Identifying the course a raindrop takes to the sea after it drips off your nose is not really that difficult: it will teach you a lot both about God's creation, about how we have altered it—and more specifically, about the quality of the water we use and our contribution to that quality. We can't think much about our watershed without asking two crucial questions about our use of it. And the answers to those questions prompt others:

Where Does My Water Come from?

A reservoir in the mountains? What hills does it drain?

A deep well? What does the water drain from? Through what does it percolate to get to your aquifer? Is the underground water being pumped out faster than it's replenished?

A river? Where has it flowed from? What has been dumped into it upstream?

Where Does My Waste Water Go?

A septic field? Where is the septic field? Where and how far does it drain? Could I separate "gray water" and use it on my lawn or garden?

A sewage system? Is the sewage treated? How much? What is done with the solid waste? Where is the liquid waste dumped? Should it be further processed? Would I want the intake of my water system downstream from the outflow of my sewage system?

The septic version of the Golden Rule: Drain unto others what you would want pumped unto you!

What Can I Do?

An exercise like the above should help us see that we are deeply involved in water quality. We are immediately concerned with what goes into us and are immediately responsible for what goes from us into the water. We are either protecting water or polluting it. Here are some specific ways in which you can protect the quality of water.

Make sure that your sewage is adequately treated. What constitutes "adequate" treatment is, of course, a matter of debate. A surprising number of North American cities, especially those by the ocean, discharge sewage wastes untreated into the sea, and the people responsible argue that the wastes are adequately dispersed and do no damage. But clearly it's a bad habit to use pure water as a dispersal for our waste.

Most urban communities have at least "primary" sewage treatment, which physically removes solid matter but releases much organic waste back into rivers. Increasing numbers of cities have "secondary" treatment, which biologically removes most of the organic waste but is less successful at removing dissolved chemicals: nitrates, phosphates, and heavy metals. Only a very few communities have the very expensive "tertiary" treatment plants, which remove the rest of the impurities. *People who care about creation should support the upgrading of their sewage systems.*

Keep untreatable materials out of your sewage system. Secondary treatment does a pretty good job of dealing with normal biological wastes. The problem therefore is the other things we dump down our drains and toilets: paint, toxic cleaners, oil, and so on. We talk elsewhere about recycling motor oil, which is notoriously difficult to filter out of water. Paint should either be used, stored (forever), or taken to a hazardous waste facility. It should never simply be "dumped," either down a drain or on the ground. The same is true for many cleaning agents, including paint thinners and cleaners.

Another major problem continues to be high-phosphate detergents, which act as fertilizing agents in the lakes and streams where they end up. The result is "eutrophication," a rapid growth of microscopic plants which take oxygen from the water and kill most of the other life. But you can switch to phosphate-free detergents.

Reduce acid rain. Some of the byproducts of coal-burning power plants and automobile engines (namely, sulphur and nitrogen oxides) enter the atmosphere and fall out eventually—sometimes hundreds of miles from their source—in the form of acid rain or snow. The accumulated effect has poisoned the life in thousands of lakes. It seems to be responsible for the death of whole forests, specially in the Eastern U.S. and Canada.

This seems like too vast a problem for the individual to deal with. But you can do two things. First, make every effort to reduce your energy consumption and the amount you drive your car. And when you do drive, make sure that emission control devices are operating properly. Collectively, those changes could make a huge impact.

Second, support government controls on acid-producing emissions. As the health of creation continues to decline—in part as the result of government policies (or lack of them)—it may be a stewardly duty to change some of our traditional political allegiances.

PROTECT FARMS

The only sustainable city—and this, to me, is the indispensable ideal and goal—is a city in balance with its countryside: a city, that is, that would live off the net ecological income of its supporting region, paying as it goes all its ecological and human debts.
—Wendell Berry, "Out of Your Car, Off Your Horse,"
The Atlantic Monthly, February 1991, 62.

It is easy to be sentimental about farms, to regard them as quaint reminders of some earlier era: Old MacDonald with his loud menagerie; or Grant Wood's "American Gothic" woman and man with pitchfork, posed dourly in front of their church-windowed house. But when we associate "farm" with "old-fashioned," we are making an enormous—and rather arrogant—error: that is, the assumption that we no longer depend on the farm to provide us our food.

That mistake is associated with several others. One of them is the attitude that we have solved the problem of production and no longer depend on an agri-culture. We unwisely conclude that a way of life associated with the rhythms of the seasons and the health of the soil is irrelevant in a food-producing world characterized by big machines and heavy use of chemicals.

A more subtle error says that the ideal "nature" is the earth untouched by human activity. There are many good reasons to preserve wilderness. But it is a mistake to assume that a wilderness condition defines the ideal human relationship to the land, for it is not a relationship at all but a kind of exclusion of relationship.

We need therefore to actively support the farm—not the large agribusiness enterprises that have forced more and more people into the city, but the small family farm raising a mixture of vegetable and animal crops on a scale that allows land, plants, and animals to be known and cared for.

In chapter eight we described various ways to support local growers. We can also support legislation that protects agricultural land. Farmland near cities is under pressure for uses other than farming. Often land is taxed at the rate of its "highest and best use." Various creative solutions—such as agricultural land reserves and municipal purchase of development rights—have kept taxes down and farmers on the land near the cities, where they are most needed.

We should also discourage attempts to remove services from rural communities in the name of efficiency and centralization. The farmland of North America is dotted with abandoned schoolhouses, empty churches, dying towns. Sometimes the demise of these small communities was inevitable and unavoidable, but often they died because of poor planning and bad decisions. To combine three or four healthy small schools into one large one because students will have access to more labs, computers, and gyms is usually to confuse education (which involves relationships with people and places) with training (the imparting of technical knowledge which can be done anywhere).

We need to support, and be willing to be a part of, small towns and small rural communities. We need to say no to the malls and super-stores that put small stores out of business. These diverse small towns and businesses nourish and encourage small farms.

The following books contain thoughtful reflections on our dependence on farms and suggestions for keeping healthy those agricultural roots of culture. Berry in particular writes from a Christian perspective.

Wendell Berry, *A Continuous Harmony* (New York: Harvest Books, 1975); *The Unsettling of America* (San Francisco: Sierra Club Books, 1977); *What Are People For?* (San Francisco: North Point Press, 1990); *Home Economics* (San Francisco: North Point Press, 1987); *The Gift of Good Land* (San Francisco: North Point Press, 1981).

Wes Jackson, Wendell Berry, Bruce Colman, *Meeting the Expectations of the Land: Essays in Sustainable Agriculture and Stewardship* (San Francisco: North Point Press, 1984).

Robert Clark, ed. *Our Sustainable Table* (San Francisco: North Point Press, 1990).

PROTECT FAMILIES

Marriage and family are a tribute paid to earth, to the tides, cycles, and needs of the body and of bodily persons; to the angularity and difficulties of the individual psyche; to the dirty diapers, dirty dishes, and endless noise and confusion of the household. It is the entire symbolic function of marriage and family to remind us that we come from dust and will return to dust, that we are part of the net of earth and sky....

—Michael Novack, "The Family out of Favor," *Harper's Magazine*, April 1976, 40.

The family has been called "the key link in the social chain of being" (Emil Durkheim), "God's first base of morality" (John Perkins), "the basic institution of society" (Brigitte and Peter Berger). Or as T.S. Eliot puts it, "Home is where one starts from." And in caring for creation, our first lessons come in the family.

Early in biblical history God himself makes clear that the

family is where the lessons of life begin: "These commandments that I give you today are to be upon your hearts.
Impress them on your children. Talk about them when you
sit at home and when you walk along the road, when you lie
down and when you get up" (Dt 6:6-7).

The commandments are God's code of behavior, his rule
book for living in creation. This code lies at the heart of faith,
society, and the survival of Jewish culture. So it was not left
for Sabbath lessons for adults. Constantly, in the home, from
the beginning, these lessons were to be taught, so that when
the children grew old the lessons would be habits of life.

Caring for creation starts with such everyday habits. Few of
us have the chance anymore to teach or learn regular habits
through chores such as milking cows and feeding chickens.
But even in the city we have chores for creation: sorting recy-
clables, smashing cans, hanging clothes to dry, turning off
the lights, turning off the water while we brush our teeth.
Little habits that we learn and live at home will save habitat,
water, farms, and families.

Yet we might ask why the family should be saddled with
teaching the basic lessons of life. Why not the church, the
day-care center, the school, or the Scout group? Certainly
such groups can and do support and help, but the principles
of ecology help us see why they are not enough. Through
our family we are involved in a net of relationships. We are
each different on all levels of our being, yet we are ines-
capably meshed with each other. As Thomas Howard puts it
in his superb book on the family, *Splendor in the Ordinary:*

No one supposes that these four or five or six people are a
select breed, tailored to get along with each other perfectly, or picked because they are better than anyone else.
Rather, it is as though the great lesson in love which we all
must learn sooner or later has been made obvious, easy,
and natural by being carried along in the arms of sheer
biology. It is easier and more obvious and natural for six

people bound this way to learn the lessons than for six people who are trying to set up a commune, say, to learn the same thing. The commune is a brave experiment, but the wheels drive heavily eventually.[1]

But how can the family be a place where the lessons of love and caring are "obvious, easy, and natural"? The "arms of sheer biology" drop more often than they carry, hit more than they hug. The "easiness" is not due to a cheap grace of God giving us smooth sailing over rough seas. Rather, the family is a place to learn these lessons precisely because we can't escape the problems.

Anything we do affects the rest of the family and the rest of creation. We can never run away from the fact that we are part of our family, and what may be even more important, our family is a part of us. We may refuse to learn the lessons of love and caring; we may even run away in body and soul from our family. But this one group of people about whom we have no choice is the easy, obvious, natural—in fact the only—place to really begin the lessons of caring.

"Love your mother," says the poster with a view of the earth from space. We should read a double message there. If we care for our *real* mother (and father, brother, sister) when she is degraded by sickness or old age, when she is dependent on us, when she needs attentive, constant, observant care, we'll have learned much to help us love "Mother Earth." Here then are some ways that we can, through the family, be more careful of creation.

Stay Married. "… for parents merely to remain married is itself an act of disobedience and an insult to the spirit of a throwaway culture in which continuity has little value."[2] Thus says Neil Postman in his book *The Disappearance of Childhood.* It is the height of irony that many who are concerned with stewardship of creation exercise such poor stewardship of their spouses, families, and children. Separation of parents

Here we approach a cruel irony. Many of the most ardent defenders of creation are at the same time ardent advocates of abortion as the only sure means of limiting population. Their argument is that too many humans will do irreparable damage to the whole planet.

Such an attitude is well-intentioned. It rises not only out of a concern for the well-being of the earth, but out of a genuine concern for the unwanted children of unwanted pregnancies—and the damage done to many who try to terminate those pregnancies illegally (a major third-world health problem). The unchecked growth of human population *is* a problem.

But more than the rest of creation, human creatures never come in the abstract or the general: they are unique beings, needing care because each one is, potentially, a caretaker of creation. It is crucial that we educate this generation into a moderate and conserving use of the earth. For the damage done to creation in the relatively wealthy "first world" is far greater than the damage done by poor and unwanted humans anywhere.

We should never let alarm at the sheer numbers of humanity turn us against individual men and women, however small, unformed, and defenseless. But neither should we assume that God's purpose for creation is to wipe out its diversity to make room for a steadily growing humanity. Sometimes we come dangerously close to saying, "Destroy the family to save the earth." That attitude is no closer to the truth than the one that says, "Destroy the earth to nourish the family." We need to make earthkeepers of our children, and the best place for that is the family.

does suggest to children that even they can be discarded (as their parents have discarded each other), and that attitude sinks deep into the psyche. (And a not insignificant burden on creation is added by the proliferation of living places required by solitary people who once were married.)

Develop a Long-Term Relationship with Children: Mary Catherine Bateson (daughter of anthropologist Margaret Mead), said it very well: "We need to involve ourselves with the life of at least one child... so that we, looking at the child, can reflect on the vast network needed to give that child a future, so that we can build up in our imagination the sense of all the other human beings and all the natural forces interlocked in support of and care for the child."[3] Our care for creation is grounded in the future through children. For the same reason Jeremiah told the disconsolate exiles in Babylon, "Marry and have sons and daughters."

Involve Children in Reducing, Reusing, Recycling. The family is the best place to begin the habits of care and sustaining that we all need to learn. The goal is for the children not to have to *unlearn* wasteful attitudes when they get older.

Make Things with Children. One of the best ways to get children interested in the possibilities of creation, and detached from the hard sell of an inescapable consumer culture, is to involve them very early in experience of making things. (See chapter four, "Make It.")

Take Regular Walks with Children. There are two advantages to this. One is that you can show the children things that they might miss and lay the groundwork for a knowledge of how creation works in your neighborhood. The other is that children will show you things *you* have missed. As G.K. Chesterton said, "... we have sinned and grown old, and our Father is younger than we."[4]

PART FOUR

SUMMER

THINGS TO DO

- ☉ Take on Adam's first full-time job: "name" the animals—and the rest of God's created world—by knowing it well.
- ☉ Invest in some good guidebooks to help your family "name creation."
- ☉ Study up on the physical history of where you are living as a way to gain perspective on what's happening to it now.
- ☉ Find the answers to "Twenty Questions about Your Place."
- ☉ Make your home and church places for "re-membering" creation.
- ☉ Learn the human history of where you live: from farmers, fishermen, craftsmen, and native people; find how the business of living life has been carried on.
- ☉ Take trains rather than planes at least for family trips—see creation and save the railroads.
- ☉ Ride bikes: save fuel and get a good—free—workout.
- ☉ WALK.
- ☉ As a vacation alternative, consider volunteer work in another country.
- ☉ Avoid vacations which exploit the people and resources of other regions.
- ☉ Explore the created world as well as the cultural world of places you visit.
- ☉ Visit the *local* church of your choice when on holiday.
- ☉ Choose recreations which re-create your joy in creation.
- ☉ Follow the camper's maxim: always leave a place in better shape than you found it.
- ☉ Encourage mission groups you and your church support to include healing of creation in their Good News.
- ☉ See your pet dog, cat, or goldfish as an opportunity to get to know another part of God's creation.
- ☉ Don't buy or use products that threaten wild things (an example: look for the "dolphin safe" symbol on your tuna can).

⊙ Insist that at least half of the income of any relief or environmental group you belong to go toward direct action rather than to administrative or informational costs.

⊙ Become involved as an active voting Christian member of a national, international, and/or local environmental organization.

⊙ Encourage local stores to carry creation-caring products.

⊙ Let your plastic money care for creation: use affinity cards that support worthwhile causes.

⊙ Give a "tithe" of your garden—or backyard—to those who don't have the opportunity to have a garden.

⊙ Remember the meaning in the menial: each act of caring is not just daily drudgery, but a beginning of the new creation.

⊙ Keep singing: "Praise with elation, praise every morning, God's re-creation of the new day!"

⊙ "Remember the Sabbath day" as a weekly celebration of the goodness of creation and Creator.

MEDITATION

Vacation and Re-creation

What we call the beginning is often the end
And to make an end is to make a beginning,...
We shall not cease from exploration
And the end of all our exploring
Will be to arrive where we started
And know the place for the first time.
　　　　　　　—T.S. Eliot, "Little Gidding"

Because the Holy Ghost over the bent world broods....
　　　—Gerard Manley Hopkins, "God's Grandeur"

○

IN THE TRADITIONAL CHURCH CALENDAR over half the year is one season: "Trinity," which stretches from Pentecost Sunday to the beginning of Advent. Like most things about the church year (at least on the human level), this is mainly coincidence, and it probably bothers people with a strong taste for symmetry: why should Christmas and Easter, the main events of the church year, be crowded into the first half, and the rest of the year be a long stretch in which nothing much happens?

Yet this asymmetry matches history, both cosmic and human. The universe itself, in its Spirit-led unfolding, is quirky, odd, and asymmetrical in the extreme. Physicists who think about such things have long been interested in the asymmetry of time: it only runs one way, and is fundamentally irreversible. Combined with the second law of thermodynamics which says that the universe is running down, cooling off, falling apart, and becoming more disordered, we are led to

203

the implication that both time and the universe had a beginning and will come to an end. This conclusion is highly embarrassing for secular man.

Terrestrial history is the same, of course. Geologically and biologically it is full of "singularities": volcanoes, earthquakes, meteor-strikes. They are not ordinary events; they happen so seldom as to be *almost* never. Yet they set things on a new course.

Human history is the same. It goes on, day after day, year after year, through its cycles of springtime and harvest, birth and death, the rise and decline of civilizations. But singularities happen, and events take a new turn, fraught with danger and possibility.

We could pick out a handful of such singular occurrences: the discovery of the "new world" by the old, for example, or various inventions such as writing, printing, and the atomic bomb. But the greatest singularity, different from all the rest, is the Incarnation, God's entrance into human history in Jesus. That the world had been irrevocably changed was not obvious at first, but now we recognize the centrality of the life of Jesus whenever we write a date.

The birth, life, and death of Jesus, those main events we celebrate in the church year, describe the singularity in creation that tells us what it is all about, the hint midway through the story that tells where it is headed. Scripture gives us various glimpses of that goal, but not many. In Ephesians Paul speaks of all things being summed up or recapitulated in Christ; and again he speaks of creation standing on tiptoe in "eager expectation" for the revealing of the sons of God. Presumably he is speaking of a redeemed humanity, living out its redemption. That human destiny is eternal, and that it does not leave creation behind, we are certain. But how that fits with entropy, the running down of time, we have no idea.

What is clear, however, is that most of life is ordinary, humdrum, everyday, and that God chooses to work in small ways and subtle ways. We know that he can suddenly turn water into wine, but usually he woos the vine from the ground; the grape from the vine, the sun, and the water; the wine from the grape. We have only dim glimpses of the beginning of creation, but we do know that the miracle of creation proceeds "normally." In Psalm 104 we see the daily round of creatures seeking their food in "natural" ways; but ultimately the food comes from God: "These all look to you to give them their food at the proper time" (Ps 104:27). And of all creatures the psalmist writes, "When you send your Spirit, they are created, and you renew the face of the earth" (Ps 104:30).

Passages like this form the foundation of a venerable Christian doctrine, that of the "Creator Spirit." It describes God's sustaining gifts through the everyday processes of creation. Sometimes we speak casually of "providence" and "the providential," but even then we are referring to the sustaining creativity of the Spirit of God.

We began this book by thinking about the symbolism of the cross and the circle. Many people in our day of increased environmental awareness have discovered something of the miracle of God's providence, of what medieval theologians called the *Creator Spiritus*: they glimpse the miracle of God's actions in the day-to-day cycles of creation. But they often miss the Spirit at the center of those cycles, whose source is God's word. It was spoken at the beginning in creation, and spoken again in Jesus for our salvation.

That long season of the church year which we call "Trinity" is also associated with the Holy Spirit: the Creator Spirit who hovered over the face of the waters, who gives all things their food, and who, through Christ, bears witness with our spirit.

In this section we consider some of the ways in which we can recognize God's actions in the everyday, in the "time being" of our lives. Summer is for many a time of vacation, a time of re-creation, a time to step back from obsessive routines of work to look more deeply at the ordinary life of creation. Those vacations can put us more in touch with the

Creator; unfortunately they are just as likely to distance us from him and his works.

So in this concluding part of the book we speak first of getting to know our own place: the "here" where we live day to day. But we also speak of getting to know other places, even other cultures and countries. The "there" may seem exotic to us, but it is home for other people.

Finally we will consider some of the ways in which our daily and ordinary actions can extend our backyard into the whole human world. We conclude by looking at ways in which observance of the Sabbath, that almost-forgotten celebration of the completion of creation, can help us participate more fully in the kingdom of the Creator.

TEN

Here: Learning to Be at Home

To be rooted is perhaps the most important and least-recognized need of the human soul. —Simone Weil, *The Need for Roots*

❂

W E HAVE SAID A GREAT DEAL in this book about creation, the pressures on it, and how we ought to care for it. But we have usually spoken of creation in general. And of course, creation is never "in general," it is always particular. When it's an abstraction, it's easier to treat as mere raw material. We need mines, landfills, and reservoirs, but we are often too casual about the ridge, the valley, the marsh we destroy to have those things.

We are more careful of the little and large bits of creation placed directly (and indirectly) into our care when we know them well. In the pages that follow we suggest doing that in four ways: by naming, by knowing, by re-membering, and by learning from "the elders"—those who have lived a long time in a place and know it well.

NAME CREATION

When Jacob awoke from his sleep, he thought, "Surely the Lord is in this place, and I was not aware of it." He was afraid and said, "How awesome is this place! This is none other than the house of God; this is the gate of heaven."... He called that place Bethel [house of God].   —Genesis 28: 16-17, 19a

◉

We moderns are probably more casual about giving names than any people have ever been. To all other peoples, naming things is not the mere casting of an arbitrary label, but a way of knowledge and power. Naming is taken seriously in the Bible: the first (and only!) task we see Adam perform in Eden is the naming of the beasts. The wording of that account is significant. "Now the Lord God had formed out of the ground all the beasts of the field and all the birds of the air. He brought them to the man to see what he would name them; and whatever the man called each living creature, that was its name" (Gn 2:19).

One gets the definite impression here of a kind of divine curiosity, as though the Creator did not know in advance what Adam his steward would make of the things he had made. We also glimpse here something of the freedom and power that God has given us. The extent of this power becomes clearer as we look more closely at what naming meant, not only in the ancient Hebrew world but to almost all premodern people.

What Naming Does. To name something is first of all to *know it.* Thus one cannot name casually or quickly, but only after study and reflection.

To name something is also to have power over it: thus the various folk tales in which someone's true name is kept concealed, lest he who discovers it have power over him. In naming the animals—presumably, through intimate knowledge of them—Adam is exercising his rightful dominion.

Yet naming is not only knowledge and power on the part of the namer; it is also a kind of liberation for the thing named. It enables a thing to become fully itself, to enter for the first time into its created purpose.

All of these dimensions of naming are still present, but we leave them to scientists and artists, and thus sidestep our responsibility and privilege as individuals. But creation waits to be named—that is, to be really *known* by us. Here are some suggestions for that kind of knowledge.

Ways of Naming.

Draw it. Before a name can mean anything, we have to learn to see the thing it means. How do we learn to see? Perhaps the best way is to draw. Most of us assume that we can't draw, though when we were children we knew better. In any case, the point of the drawing isn't to "make a picture": it's to increase our knowledge of the thing we're looking at. Nothing makes one more aware of the complexity and design of a created thing—leaf, rock, tree, cloud, bird—than to try to put it on paper.

So carry a notebook and a pencil, for you are entrusted with the high task of knowing and naming God's creatures. A simple hint: see the whole form first and sketch it. Begin a leaf with an oval, circle, or triangle; then subdivide it into the appropriate created distinctives. (There's an earthkeeping lesson here: most of our problems in caring for creation come from our looking at the parts before the whole.)

Write it. You can draw by writing too, and this is getting closer to naming: trying to grasp a thing with words. Words can do things that drawings can't, and for some of us they're less daunting. With words you can indicate the passage of time; you can also begin to connect the thing with your feelings and speculate on what it means in God's plan. Think of these creation-based writings as your own psalms. (Many of the biblical psalms also begin with things in creation.) Or include them in letters to friends. One of the best things a letter can do is share your experience of creation and Creator with someone else.

Learn the names. Get to know, by name, the flowers, ferns, mosses, mushrooms, animals, trees, and rocks in your area. You'll do this on three levels. In drawing and describing them you have come to know them and given *your* name for them. That's the first and most important level.

On the second level, it's good to know their conventional names as well: blood-root, maidenhair, chantrel, sassafras, mule deer, yellow-bellied sapsucker. The names themselves are strange, and they let you enter the leisurely conversation with creation which our ancestors had.

Finally, there is good reason to learn the scientific names, if for no other reason than that it gives you tools for being precise in your naming. It also allows you entry into the vast botanical and zoological literature of what we know about creatures. At this point, of course, we're entering science. But science, like art, is also a way of naming.

Use guidebooks. As an aid to all of these ways of giving names to creation, build up a small library of guidebooks on trees, flowers, rocks, and so on. Just about every aspect of creation, at least in North America and Europe, is covered by such books, and they are excellent ways of getting to know the creatures with which you share your place. Be sure to get guidebooks with the pictures and text side-by-side; it saves a lot of flipping around. And though photographs are beautiful, drawings are more helpful in identification.

KNOW YOUR PLACE

Some unwonted, taught pride diverts us from our original intent, which is to explore the neighborhood, view the landscape, to discover at least where it is that we have been so startlingly set down, if we can't learn why. —Annie Dillard, *Pilgrim at Tinker Creek*

> May 18.... I do not think I have ever seen anything more beautiful than the bluebell I have been looking at. I know the beauty of our Lord by it. It is mixed of strength and grace, like an ash tree. The head is strongly drawn over and arched down like a cutwater. The lines of the bell strike and overlie this, rayed but not symmetrically, some lie parallel. They look steely against paper, the shades lying between the bells and behind the cocked petal-ends...
>
> —Gerard Manley Hopkins, journal entry. *Poems and Prose*, selected by W.H. Gardner (Middlesex, England: Penguin Books, 1963), 120.

By naming we begin to know individual creatures. But we can't go very far with naming and knowing individuals before we begin to realize that they (and we) are part of a much larger picture. It's a delight to learn that larger picture and our place in it. It's also a necessity if we're going to do a very good job of caring for it.

Some of these questions you can't answer without getting to know your place a lot better, which means some snooping around. We suggested earlier that a very good way to begin getting to know your place is to explore your watershed, big and little. Watersheds are based on the shape of the land: and the land where you live is itself shaped by a variety of slow processes. Understanding them gives you a deeper knowledge of the place and some of the means God uses to create.

It's hard to be abstract about this, so we list some of the places we have lived in the years since our marriage. Make your own list.

In northern Illinois: the fertile outwash plain of the last great ice sheet, overlain (if you know where to look for it) by the features left by a receding glacier: moraines and eskers. When we were in college there an excavation for construction uncovered the complete skeleton of a mastodon, which had waded too deeply into a post-glacial bog. The soil is fertile, but increasingly covered by the rapidly-advancing glacier of Chicago and its suburbs.

In upstate New York: hillier country, where the marks of the receded ice are more evident. We lived on the outskirts of a city, on one of many drumlins: great humped ridges of glacial debris, steep on one side, gradual on the other, carved by the glacial flow. (Our drumlin made great sledding—slow and tame down the long axis, fast and scary down the sides.)

In a little walnut woods near our house we found, among the native limestone ledges, a boulder of bright pink granite. This was probably carried by the ice from the Precambrian shield, the vast slab of old rock that caps and characterizes much of eastern Canada, and which one Canadian poet describes as "strength broken by strength and still strong." We've carried two chunks of the rock around with us ever since, for doorstops, bookends, and a reminder of the drumlins.

Further to the south, where the glacier carved deep valleys in the soft limestone, we found waterfalls pouring over limestone slabs full of fossils. We still have fossil-filled rocks in our house from those hills.

In Seattle: again, a city built on glacial debris, but this time on an arm of the Pacific Ocean. Across that arm, a range of mountains where the glaciers still dig. To the east, more mountains, the northern part of the Cascades: glaciers, lakes, the whole range heavy with rain or snow three-forths of the year, nourishing an incredibly rich, dense forest that is being cut down and hauled off with a speed much greater than anything the glaciers accomplished.

Later we lived on a big island in the same inland sea, near a wave-cut bluff of debris. There one day our daughter found a curiously-shaped stone, like a broken piece of pipe, that turned out to be part of a mastodon tusk.

Then, for a few years, in southern Oregon, in the southern part of the Cascades: gentler hills, south of where the glaciers ever came. Here the forces that shaped the place were mainly volcanic: ancient lava flows and eruptions; the rock basalt, pumice, obsidian (sometimes shaped exquisitely, by long-gone natives, into arrowheads).

One morning we found fine dust on our windshield from the explosion of Mount St. Helens, three-hundred miles north. Another time a mild earthquake made our water flow milky with rock dust for a day, for it came from a spring that gushed out beneath basalt columns after sinking through old cracks and conduits of stone.

Then to Vancouver, another city by the sea built partly on the leftovers from receding ice and partly on the delta of a huge river. We write this from an island fifteen miles away from that city, formed of tilted layers of sandstone that slant into the straits on one side and on the other side fall in steep cliffs. Between the sandstone ridges are narrow valleys filled with beaver ponds, alder, cedar trees, and skunk cabbage.

One of those valleys was cleared early in this century and turned into a farm. Our house sits between the valley and a little cove, where people have dug clams for thousands of years and thrown the shells in piles: the drain field from our septic tank is in a midden of old shells several feet thick.

These places from our life story are no more or less significant than the places you live. Every "here" has a long, rich, often mysterious history: human, biological, geological. We can understand and care better for a place by knowing its past and its connections.

There are many other features of your place that are worth knowing: the weather and where it comes from; the plants and when they bloom; the animals and what they eat. Here's a little quiz that might help you to get to know your place better:

Where on the earth are you?
(Twenty Questions about Your Place)
Adapted from Bill Duvall and George Sessions, *Deep Ecology*[1]

1. Trace the water you drink from precipitation to tap.
2. How many days until the moon is full (plus or minus a couple of days)?
3. Describe the soil around your home.
4. What were the primary subsistence techniques of the culture(s) that lived in your area before you?
5. Name five native edible plants in your area and their season(s) of availability.
6. From what direction do winter storms generally come in your region?
7. Where does your garbage go?
8. How long is the growing season where you live?
9. Name five trees in your area. Are any of them native? If you can't name names, describe them.
10. Name five resident and any migratory birds in your area.
11. What is the land use history by humans in your area during the past century?
12. What primary geological event or process influenced the land form where you live?
13. From where you are reading this, point north.
14. What spring wildflower is consistently among the first to bloom where you live?
15. What kinds of rocks and minerals are found in your area?
16. How many people live next door to you? What are their names?
17. How much gasoline do you use a week, on the average?
18. What developed and potential energy resources are in your area?
19. What plans are there for large development in your area?
20. What is the largest wild region in your area?

RE-MEMBER CREATION

Remember is the opposite of *forget*. And we do indeed need to remember, as individuals and cultures, much that we have forgotten about the creation around us. But "re-member" is also the opposite of *dismember*. In various ways we have torn creation apart, and we need to work at putting it back together again. A dramatic example from a Christian in India might make clearer some of the possibilities for things we can do close to home.

Dr. Fritschi is an Indian leprosy doctor who grew up in the Nilgiri hills and has spent much of his adult life near Karigiri in Tamil Nadu, in southern India. The place is a hot, largely barren plain, suffering like much of the third world from deforestation, overgrazing, and a drastically falling water table. A long time ago it was fertile and well-watered, but now most of the region is semi-desert: the monsoon rains run rapidly off the stony hills because most of the vegetation has been degraded through a growing population's constant search for firewood and goat fodder.

Dr. Fritschi is an expert in reconstructive surgery on victims of leprosy. These people's limbs are malformed because they no longer feel pain, and thus go on using injured parts of the body when they should give them time to recover. "We're probably the only hospital where the doctors are glad when the patients are in pain," Dr. Fritschi told us. "In leprosy patients when there's pain, there's hope." We saw a woman who could use her hands again and a man who could walk again on what had once been useless stumps, both through delicate neurosurgery. These people had been literally "re-membered" by Dr. Fritschi, who had felt the pain *for them* and known what to do about it.

Dr. Fritschi's spare time concern is strangely like his job: rebuilding the landscape of the hospital. He has fenced the grounds to keep the foraging goats out; he has built numerous retaining dams to slow the run-off and build up the soil.

He has planted trees chosen for their role in a nearly vanished ecosystem. When the voracious white ants kept eating the leaves that fell from the trees, hindering the build-up of humus, he introduced pangolins, native spiny ant-eaters. (Unfortunately, hungry neighbors persisted in killing the pangolins for their edible tail.) We saw pictures of the hospital when it was built forty years ago: the stone buildings stood out squarely on a stony, treeless plain. But today when you approach from any direction you don't even see the buildings; you see only the green mound of the re-membered forest, which now surrounds the hospital. The air around the hospital is cool and moist, the walks deeply shaded by big trees.

In North America most of our landscapes and ecosystems are not yet so obviously dismembered as was this hospital's. But they too are badly in need of Christians who will begin the slow, thoughtful task of restoration. Here are some small things you can do:

Restore Native Vegetation. When landscaping your house or church, work at reconstructing the original vegetation of the area. This will be slow, uncertain work. But in doing it you are restoring not only plants but habitat for insects, birds, and animals that have formed part of the living fabric of the place.

Create Habitat for Endangered Species. Deliberately create environments to attract and nurture rare and endangered species. Various species of birds and butterflies find normal habitat on both ends of their migration dwindling. A simple thing like a birdfeeder can add considerably to a bird's chances of surviving in an area.

Preserve Native Ecosystems. If you have an area in your community or city that preserves native species in a largely intact ecosystem, see that it doesn't get regarded as simply another convenient building site. This is especially true for prairie ecosystems, of which very few remain. Consider raising funds to have those areas preserved. Nature Trust and Nature Conservancy are two organizations that work with communities to raise money to preserve important areas.

Build Trails. See that trails are built in threatened natural areas. There is a trade-off here, of course: trails attract people who do damage. But trails also attract people who will be concerned about a place. Trails are a way of letting a place enter into the awareness of a community, without ceasing to be itself.

Make Your Church a Place for "Re-membering" Creation. Work to make your church and your home a "creation awareness center": a place for "re-membering" creation in every sense of the word. Here are two things you might do:

—Make a quiet garden area on church property where native plants and wildlife can flourish. See chapter seven section on flowers for information on gardens that attract birds and butterflies.

—Make information on local trails and natural areas available *through* the church, and recommend clean-up and trail construction projects as possible activities for church groups. This is not watering down the gospel but broadening it: reminding us that we are the stewards of creation.

LEARN FROM THE OLD ONES

The ground says, It is the Great Spirit that placed me here. The Great Spirit tells me to take care of the Indians, to feed them aright. The Great Spirit appointed the roots to feed the Indians on. The water says the same thing. The Great Spirit directs me, Feed the Indians well. The grass says the same thing, Feed the Indians well. The ground, water and grass say, The Great Spirit has given us our names. We have these names and hold these names. The ground says, The Great Spirit has placed me here to produce all

*that grows on me, trees and fruit. The same way the ground says,
It was from me man was made. The Great Spirit, in placing men
on the earth, desired them to take good care of the ground and to
do each other no harm....*

—Young Chief, a Cayuse Indian, in 1855,
Touch the Earth by T.C. McLuhan

◉

In "The New World"—which includes North and South
America, Australia, and New Zealand—most of us are transplanted, living in a place different from the one that shaped
our culture and language. So we can and should learn from
the people who grew up with the place: the native peoples
who lived in rough harmony with it. What plants are edible?
With what could we build shelter? What stories are associated
with particular hills, lakes, rocks?

This is information known by the people whom we have,
for the most part, supplanted or assimilated—many times
cruelly. Often such information has died with those people,
but it ought to be part of our stewardship of creation to learn
the names they gave places and plants.

The fact that the stories and names are often related to
gods, demons, and spirits should not bother us greatly: the
wisdom is genuine, as is the deep sense (present in almost all
native peoples), that behind the haze of legend this is creation, and there is a Creator, a "great Spirit" whom we should
honor. We were able to tell the native peoples (as Paul told
the Athenians) something more of that "unknown God." But
we need to be humble enough to recognize that our words
about that God of love have often been betrayed by our
actions. And we need the humility as well to recognize that
native people have often been more respectful of both creation and Creator, and thus they have much to teach us.

Most of us are cut off even from those of our own culture
who settled our land. Often, of course, our reverence for
"pioneers" and "old-timers" is misplaced, for they sometimes

were among the most destructive of creation. But in many parts of the new world communities have managed to live in a stable and sustainable relationship with the land. Most of these are agricultural communities, but on the East coast we find some based on fishing. These people can be valuable resources, experts in place-related stewardship.

Our own parents, grandparents, great-grandparents, aunts, and uncles embody wisdom about creation and its care that should not be lost. Most of us have relatives who can remember the first time they saw a car or an airplane, or heard a radio. They have seen a technological transformation of a rural nation to an urban one. What that means in human terms is that skills that once were common knowledge—plowing with a horse, drying vegetables, spinning wool—are guarded by a few specialists or locked up in the memories of people who think their bypassed knowledge is useless.

Along with skills, we need our elders' memories of creation: of the forest that used to grow on the site of the suburb; of the hundreds of thousands of ducks that used to feed where now only a few hundred come; of the vanished clarity of streams. We profit from these pictures not just for nostalgia, but as a painter can profit from a photograph of a canvas he hopes to restore.

An important part of caring for creation, therefore, is listening to our elders. Here are some suggestions:

—Talk to your older relatives about local areas as they knew them in their youth. They may have unwittingly contributed to the decline of the region's health, but we still have much to learn from their knowledge and skills.

—Read histories of your place. Look especially for people who were able to see, appreciate, and wonder at the created world. Local museums are a valuable resource here: not just as a record of the past, but as a source of clues for a future.

—Seek out and listen to those farmers, fishermen, and craftsmen who have maintained a continuous tradition of stewardship in a place. Honor them and what they have to say—and record it and write it down.

—Seek out, listen to, and support local members of native communities—especially those who are genuinely interested in the well of creation-knowledge that their people guard.

The Foxfire Book (in three volumes, Garden City, NY: Doubleday, 1972) grew out of a high-school project in the Appalachians in which students interviewed "old-timers." It is an excellent glimpse of a lost world in which knowledge of creation played a much greater part.

ELEVEN

There: Travel, Vacation, and Care for Creation

For still there are so many things
that I have never seen:
in every wood in every spring
there is a different green.
　　　　　—J.R.R. Tolkien, *The Fellowship of the Ring*

◉

S UMMER HAS ALWAYS BEEN a time for travel. "Vacation" means we "vacate" one place and go to another one. The pleasures and broadening benefits of travel are undeniable: we learn more about the beauty, complexity, and fragility of the earth we are to care for.

Nevertheless, our travel is a mixed blessing for the earth. The knowledge we gain is often superficial, not the sort that comes from living in a place. And when we travel we make demands on the place and people we visit, often demonstrating a wasteful standard of living which is insidiously destructive of the very place we have traveled to see.

In this chapter we consider ways in which our travel can be careful of creation: first, through lessening the impact of transportation; then, through wise visiting and study of new places and cultures; finally, through reflecting on the very

nature of sojourning, especially in the various kinds of camping.

GETTING TO A PLACE: TRANSPORTATION

> *Toad sat straight down in the middle of the dusty road, his legs
> stretched out before him, and stared fixedly in the direction of the
> disappearing motor-car. He breathed short, his face wore a placid,
> satisfied expression, and at intervals he faintly murmured "Poop-
> poop!..."*
>
> *"Glorious, stirring sight!" murmured Toad, never offering to
> move. "The poetry of motion! The real way to travel! The only
> way to travel! Here to-day—in next week to-morrow! Villages
> skipped, towns and cities jumped—always somebody else's horizon!
> O bliss! O poop-poop! O my! O my!"*
>
> —Kenneth Grahame, *The Wind in the Willows*

In North America, when we think of going somewhere
else, we almost always think of getting in the car and driving.
But the majority of the world's people will never even ride in
a car, much less own one. We need to think long and hard
about the costs to creation of the automobile, which of all
our inventions is almost certainly the most destructive of
God's earth.

Some Car Facts:

—Americans drive more than a trillion miles a year in 140
million cars, more than a third of the world's total of 400
million.

—Every gallon of gas burned combines with oxygen to produce more than twenty pounds of carbon dioxide: thus
cars are a major source of the gasses causing the "green-
house effect."

—Cars are a major source of nitrous oxide, and hence of the

acid rain that is destroying many eastern forests and lakes.

—Cars have made many of our urban areas essentially inaccessible to pedestrians, thus limiting the possibility of real community in the city.

—Parking, highways, and the dispersion made possible by the automobile have caused cities to grow much larger, often devouring the agricultural land that supported them in the first place.

—Because cars insulate us from creation, they make it easier to ignore its degradation, as well as sounds, sights, and odors.

—American transportation uses about two-thirds of the oil imported, making the nation exceptionally vulnerable (as we have witnessed several times after Mid-East political upheavals) to disruptions in its oil supply.

One of the best things we can do to practice care for creation is to drive less and use alternative methods of travel. Through such things as public transit, improvement of routes for bikers and pedestrians, and most importantly, the simple choice to drive less (a choice likely to be imposed eventually by the rising cost of fuel), we can significantly reduce the degradation of creation brought about by the automobile. (You might want to look again at the table "Energy Intensity of Transport Modes" in chapter two, p. 40.)

If You Have to Drive.

—Make sure your car is tuned up.

—When you buy another car, make fuel-efficiency a major consideration.

—If you have more than one car, reduce the number. Does your family really need two (or three)?

—Consider getting rid of your car entirely, using alternate methods ordinarily and renting a car for special needs and occasions.

—Arrange a carpool for getting to work. This is a good relationship-builder too. Some communities have a central clearing house for locating carpool partners. Some cities have a freeway traffic lane designated for transit vehicles or cars with at least three people. Support such a policy in your community.

Alternatives to Driving:

Use public transportation—bus, train, or subway. If you figure in the reading and napping you can do on bus or train, and the time you *won't* need to "unwind" from the traffic, you're usually ahead with public transit.

Cost is not a clear-cut argument against taking public transportation. If you figure all the costs of driving—including the extra insurance you pay to drive to work—you will almost certainly save money using transit.

It's important to support the establishment and expansion of public transit systems. At a dedication of a new transit station in our city recently a nosey reporter found out that none of the dignitaries there to praise the transit system had arrived by transit. Their excuses weren't very good.

For long trips take the train, instead of a plane. In terms of fuel, the train is one of the most efficient of transportation systems, and flying one of the least efficient. Of course it takes longer, but you will see more of the fine detail of creation. Passenger-rail systems are fighting for their life. They will almost certainly return as fossil fuels become scarcer and more expensive—but it's a shame to lose them in the interim. Our riding on the railroads will help keep them running.

For shorter trips ride a bike. There are 800 million bicycles in the world, outnumbering cars two to one. Bikes already meet the majority of the world's mechanized transport needs. They are the most energy-efficient form of land transportation yet developed. Bikes are nonpolluting, use only food for fuel, are good for the health of the rider, and reduce urban congestion—so much so that bikes are faster than cars in many downtown areas.

Widespread use of bikes for commuting will be helped by more bicycle paths, designated bike lanes, and education of the public. It would also be helped if workplaces would provide showers and parking places.

Whenever possible, walk. It's not only energy-efficient; it is the all-time best way to see, hear, smell, and touch God's creation.

VISITING A NEW PLACE

The human world around us has become more and more standardized. The differences among modern cities, shopping malls, or airports on different continents are mainly superficial. At the same time, transportation to anywhere in the world has become easier, and more and more North Americans are choosing to visit countries that seem exotic. Many of these countries are poor. There are good reasons for travel to the poor nations of the world, but often we don't go for those reasons.

Here are some potential problems with third-world tourism.

—Third-world tourism often exploits and oppresses local people, destroys their culture and environment, and widens the gap between the rich and poor. Permits for mega-resorts are railroaded through with little care for the carrying capacity of the land or water system. Transportation to and from the resorts, supplies, entertainment, and even many of the service people are often provided by either the country of the home corporation or imported from areas quite distant from the site.

—The profits rarely stay inside the third-world host countries. In Thailand only about ten percent of tourism profits stay in the local economy; of that, seventy-six cents from each dollar goes for import of items to support the tourist industry.

The Golden Rule, "Do unto others as you would have them do unto you," is not only about the neighbor across the street. In our choice of where to go and what to do for our holidays, we have the opportunity to show God's care on an international level.

Where shall we go?

If we want "all the comforts of home," we should probably stay home. We should, at any rate, look very carefully at our motives for going to another country. When we go to a third-world country for a "vacation" on our terms, we make far more demands for transportation, water, and space than does the average resident of that place. Our demands not only strain the over-taxed resources of the place: they contribute to the idea that this is a good way to live. When we export those models to Christians in other countries, we do great damage.

We may need to redefine "rest and relaxation." Often our pursuit of relaxation does not really bring us rest: our budgets and our bothers usually accompany us. We have a sudden empty slate, and so we finally get the cold we've been warding off, or perhaps a migraine. The best rest often comes to us in the invigorating freshness of new directions for our thinking, new visions to dream or even new concerns. Most of the time we don't need "rest and relaxation" so much as we need "reviving and renewing," something to jerk us out of the stress of our daily duties.

If we do go to another country, we need to consider staying in one place rather than trying to "do" the country. The longer we spend in one place, the more we'll be able to see through the glitz and glamour of the resorts and the tourist facade and into the life of the people and the place. Increasing numbers of Christians are using their vacation time to do short stints of work in other countries—as with "Habitat for Humanity," which builds houses for people who can't afford them.

Wherever we go we need to continually remind ourselves that the similarities we share with each person we see far outweigh the differences. All of us care for those we love; we want people to like us; we appreciate a smile; we worry about our families.

TEN QUESTIONS TO HELP US RESPECT A PLACE AND ITS PEOPLE:

1. Is my lodging owned and operated by local people?
2. Am I finding ways to learn about creation in this place?
3. Am I having an opportunity to talk in a normal conversational way about mutual concerns with anyone for whom this place is home?
4. If I am with a cruise or tour, is the waste being disposed of responsibly?
5. Does the manufacture or sale of the souvenir I bought threaten either wildlife or plantlife?
6. Did my bargaining for a good price contribute to the discrepancy of income between the rich and poor?
7. Am I contributing in any way in my trip to what is being done here to care for creation?
8. Am I showing respect for the integrity of the culture by adapting my dress?
9. Am I showing respect for the culture by using some of the local language, if only to say thank you?
10. Am I showing respect for the people by using local mannerisms—such as holding hands together and bowing when greeting someone or if a woman, covering arms and head in places of worship?

Reading: *The City of Joy,* by Dominique Lapierre (New York: Warner Books, 1985), is about Calcutta, India. It is a good eye-opener to the richness and dense texture of life in the third world. *The Ugly American,* by William Lederer and Eugene Burdick (Greenwich, CT: Fawcett Publications, Inc. 1958), is out-of-date in its pre-Vietnam political setting, but still very relevant in its cultural concerns.

KNOWING A NEW PLACE

No matter where There is, when you arrive it becomes Here.
—Muggles, *Maxims* in Carl Kendall, *The Gammage Cup*

All the suggestions on knowing your own place in the "here" section are also good ideas for getting to know any place. Treating every place as though it were home, by knowing its less-beaten tracks, its ordinary folk, its birds, trees, and flowers, is a good way to start feeling at home in another part of God's creation. And only when we have an intimate knowledge of the life of a place will we have any idea of how to care for it. In the end we may have found a new home—and certainly new friends.

Before You Go—Armchair Travel.
One of the great joys of taking a trip is the days and even months of anticipation. With a map and some guidebooks you can read your way around the place you'll be visiting. Later, when you're battling with jet lag and a bombardment of new sights, smells, and sounds, you'll be very thankful for every bit of armchair travel you crammed in.

Armchair travel is not only a great way to prepare for a visit to a strange place; it may well become a habit. We can explore Ghana or Galiano with equal ease. Whether we ever get out of the armchair or not, we will be able to seek the welfare of our neighbor's backyard more intelligently.

Get good maps. One detailed map is all you need, as much like a topographic road map as possible. (That is, it should show both natural features like hills and valleys and human features like roads and towns.) You may have to hunt a bit.

Sometimes you can find good maps in travel or hiking equipment stores.

You may be able to get a map through a country's or state's tourist information bureau, but these may be so geared to the tourist sights that the everyday places won't even show up. And though *National Geographic* maps often give an excellent feel for natural and historical features, they usually won't work for transportation use.

Read the right books. Three types of books offer three essential sorts of information.

—The "Lonely Planet" guides (published by Lonely Planet Publications), often subtitled the "travel survival kit," are just that. They are extremely practical and interestingly written. They may be the only help you get in actually exploring the countryside. Use these guides to find a place that will make a good home base for several days of walks and exploration.

—Nature Guides. You'll need a good library or an interlibrary loan for these. Try to get guides for trees, flowers, and birds. If you can't get them, settle for a coffee table picture book. Some of these are strictly tourist-trap résumés, but some, published by such groups as *National Geographic,* the Audubon Society, and the Sierra Club, can be wonderful introductions to both the diversity of natural beauty and the threats to that beauty.

—Literature. Travelogues, biographies, *National Geographic* articles, histories, and carefully chosen novels can be wonderful ways to make the country or region a tangible place. Be sure to read with your map beside you.

Check out the newspaper. Read newspapers and magazines for updates on current events and political issues that will help you understand the internal concerns and environmental problems the area is dealing with. The *Christian Science Monitor* is relatively thorough in its coverage of world news.

Its reporting is realistic rather than hyped for sensational media appeal.

Once You're There—out of Your Chair.

Get plenty of rest. Everything will be easier to cope with if you get the sleep you need. When traveling long distances by air, consider before you leave a gradual shift of your bedtime and rising time to match the clock of your destination.

Support local businesses. Many tour packages involve a complete imposition of a wealthy country on a poor one. We may think we are seeing Malaysia, or Hawaii, but our airline may own the hotel, the tour buses, the restaurant, the golf course. It may import much of the food we eat from outside the country, and (of course) receive all the profits. Ask local people where *they* eat and where *they* stay.

Support local efforts to care for creation. Try to spend part of your visit exploring a wildlife area or a conservation project. Not only will this help you become aware of others' concerns for problems in their own backyard, but your visit, indicating international interest and support, may help their cause.

Pace your life with the life of the place. By going to bed early and rising early, you can often get a fuller sense of the pattern of life in a place. The cool of the morning may be the time to climb those hills on the edge of the city and explore old ruins, see the wildlife of an area, and take part in the rhythm of another land and people.

Slow down, see more. If you really want to get to know a place, the slower you go the more you'll see. Your own feet will take you places where everyday life is going on in much the same rhythm as ours, but in beautifully different variations. Doorsteps will be swept, but they may then be dusted in an intricate chalk design; school children will eat their lunches, but they may first carefully lay out napkins, then open an intricate assortment of containers; gardens are watered, but the farmer may sing a water song in time with his hand pump.

Explore the neighborhood. Search for ways to explore the created earth as well as the cultural world. Take a bird book or a tree and flower guide with you. Explore the diversity of habitat and creatures. Being able to identify five birds, five trees, and five flowers will go a long way toward helping you know the *home* that is here. Make yourself a project of learning the twenty questions about a place from chapter ten, "Know Your Place" wherever you visit.

Go to church. Resist these objections:

— "I won't understand the service." Worship is far more than words. (Much of a sermon in Africa, for example, is in a language that is far richer than words.) And we would not think it strange at all if someone who spoke little English visited our church.

— "Why go to church when I'm on holiday?" The Bible emphasizes that corporate worship is crucial: "Do not forsake the gathering of yourselves together." Going to church in a new place helps us see the breadth and depth in the community of believers—and our need for mutual encouragement.

— "I don't know any of the people." Our faith is at the heart of who we are as persons—whether we're from India or Indiana. We are, after all, brothers and sisters in Christ, joint heirs of the kingdom of God; in communion we partake of a common meal. We are blocks from the same building, branches off the same vine, members of the same body. We may share more of what matters most with these people than with the neighbors we chat with every day. And getting to know these brothers and sisters will help us care deeply for them and for their land.

Notes from a Visit to India

Tonight we visited a Telagu-speaking church in Bombay. We went to a combined housewarming, baby dedication in what some people say is the largest slum in the world. This was not a squatter's shack, but a cement building with three small rooms, blue-painted, cool, clean. We sat on woven mats in the outer room, looking down the street to the people coming and going, to the ceaseless life of India.

We sang hymns composed in Telagu, meant to be accompanied, like Hindu chants, on tabla and harmonium. The name of Jesus was the only word I recognized in the songs. There was joy on the face of our young host and hostess. Afterwards they proudly served us rice, a goat curry, a peppery sauce, and a yogurt sauce with red onions. Perhaps twenty people—men and women, young and old, along with two well-behaved dogs, took part in the service. There is no building for this church, except the homes of the newly-baptized members. They hold their baptisms on the same beach we had walked on earlier. Most of the people here were neighbors. As we walked down from that meeting, moon rising over miles of huts, rhythms of the Telagu hymns still in my mind, the taste of coriander still on my tongue, I thought of lines from an old hymn:

> In Christ now meet both east and west
> in him meet south and north;
> all Christly souls are one in him
> throughout the whole wide earth.

SOJOURNING IN A PLACE

This thou perceivest, which makes thy love more strong,
To love that well which thou must leave ere long.
—William Shakespeare, Sonnet 73

○

Sojourn is an old-fashioned word that carries a weight of meaning. When we ask someone, "Where do you sojourn?" she will probably say where her home is. For the word does mean "make a place home." But *sojourn* contains more than a hint of "journey": it means not "home" so much as "home for awhile." So to sojourn in any place is to recognize that you might move on, that you're on a journey.

There is a paradox here: many of us find it hard to be at home anywhere. Often it is only in leaving a place (or oddly, in being *required* to be there, as an exile is) that we recognize how much it is home to us.

An old gospel song goes, "This world is not my home. I'm just a passin' through." The words can indicate an attitude that has rightly been blamed for many irresponsible actions toward creation, as though we need not care for any place we're just "passin' through." And yet we ought to name, know, and deeply care for any corner of creation where we find ourselves.

There are those today who argue that it is our rootless, transplanted European homelessness that has made us misuse this land. They argue for "bioregionalism," for reinhabiting a place, putting down roots, and becoming part of it. Those are worthy goals. But the Christian can never completely affirm them, nor can any honest man or woman. For no earthly place is completely our home. We are the only thing in nature that is *more than* nature.

Paradoxically, it is when we realize that we are only sojourners that we are apt to take better care of a place. When it's "ours" eternally, we're likely to take it for granted. When we recognize that the whole of creation is a gift and that our participation in any place may be taken away, then we are more likely to cherish that place.

Here are some suggestions for being careful sojourners.

Know the Place. Don't wait until you're "permanent" in a place to get to know its rocks, trees, flowers, birds, and seasons. Of course, we are not permanently in any place except the grave and even there, thanks to God, we wait for the resurrection. For the sake of the place where you are, be as concerned about the water, the air, and the wild things as if they were forever yours.

Use Christian Camps Well. Lots of Christian organizations have established camps or conference centers in areas of great natural beauty. It is not surprising that when people are taken out of the busy, man-made world and given a chance to see and respond to God's works in creation, they will be more likely to listen to the Creator's call to be renewed in Christ. This is a high and appropriate use of the created world, and it should be continued. But the leadership of all too many Christian camps (including some "Christian wilderness experience" programs) views creation as nothing more than a backdrop for personal encounter with God, as though the gospel had no relevance for the lake, the woods, the mountains, or the sea. Yet in their mute declaration of the glory of God, these are an essential voice in proclaiming the gospel. We should work therefore to make sure that Christian camps are places to study and appreciate what God has done in creation. And in the way they deal with food, waste, construction, and recreation, Christian camps can be places for teaching some basic principles of good stewardship of creation.

A very good Christian wilderness program oriented toward God as both Savior and Creator is "Sierra Treks," operating in the mountains of Oregon, Washington, and California. Write to it at 15097 Highway 66; Ashland, OR 97520.

Recreate Creatively. Avoid "recreations" that get between you and your experience of creation. Don't let your presence in a place be dependent on a loud motor that will destroy the very thing you're there for. Avoid activities whose main thrill is speed, noise, and a sense of having "gotten the better of" the hill, lake, or river. Ski, don't snow-mobile; canoe, don't waterski; walk, rather than motorbike. These quieter, slower ways of being a sojourner in a place are more likely to let God's work be seen and heard.

Camp with Care. "Camping" is almost a modern synonym for sojourning. It gives us a chance to grow deeply attached to a place for a few hours, days, or weeks, knowing that we will leave it, but cherishing it more for all that. For many people, camping in unspoiled creation awakens for the first time an awareness both of what God has given us and how we often mis-use it.

But camping can destroy the very thing it seeks to cherish. This is as true of rugged backcountry camping as it is of the paved campground with showers beside the freeway. Whether on the slopes of Everest, whose base camp has been degraded by the discards of climbers, or in a campground catering to motorized "campers," we miss the point if in order to serve our own comfort we diminish the very creation we have come to experience.

In general, it's good to take a place on its own terms, to bring as little of "home" with us as possible. Our goal should be to get to know a place for what it is, to leave it in better shape than it was when we arrived, and thus not to diminish it through making it more like our home. This guideline of "minimum impact camping" enables us to be more at home in a place than if we had brought home (complete with TV, stereo, microwave, and motorbike) with us.

Having spent a hard-earned sleep, you must break
    camp in the mountains
At the break of day, pulling up stakes and packing,
Scattering your ashes
And burying everything human you can't carry. Lifting
Your world now on your shoulders, you should turn
To look back once
At a place as welcoming to a later dead-tired stranger
As it was to your eyes only the other evening,
As the place you've never seen
But must hope for now at the end of a day's rough jour-
    ney:
You must head for another campsite....
  —David Waggoner, "Breaking Camp" in *Collected Poems, 1956-1976*

TWELVE

Everywhere

Go into all the world and preach the good news to all creation.
—Mark 16:15

●

WE BEGAN THIS BOOK by looking at God's earth as a whole—as those pictures from space enable us to do. But we have spent most of the time in our own backyard (or kitchen, or bathroom, or garden) looking at relatively simple things we can do for the health of the earth. Nobody can save a planet: but we might well be able to save a tree, a farm, a watershed, a family.

Nevertheless, in a healthy concern for "our place," we cannot forget our connection to the whole earth, any more than we can rest in our own salvation and forget that the gospel is a message for all things, all peoples, all places. God said "it is good" five times before he got around to us. If dominion means anything, it means doing all we can to restore that goodness. In this concluding chapter we look at the all-encompassing nature of our stewardship and at the Sabbath, that regular reminder of the goodness of all creation.

ALL PLACES

The earth is one but the world is not. We all depend on one biosphere for sustaining our lives. Yet each community, each country,

strives for survival and prosperity with little regard for its impact on others.
—The World Commission on Environment and Development, *Our Common Future*

But God has combined the members of the body and has given greater honor to the parts that lacked it, so that there should be no division in the body, but that its parts should have equal concern for each other. If one part suffers, every part suffers with it; if one part is honored, every part rejoices with it.
—1 Corinthians 12:24-26

○

Till fairly recently, a concern for the environment was considered by many—Christians included—to be a luxury of the rich. The real world problems were war, disease, poverty, hunger. The real issues had to do with "development": raising people's standards of living by building an industrial economy and a consumer society like North America's. So we have divided the world into "developed" and "developing" nations, and have defined "development" as the achievement of a society that uses creation much like we do.

The dubious term "third world" comes from dividing the world into capitalist ("first world"), communist ("second world"), and those countries that are unaligned, the "third world." Our foreign policy has been mainly shaped by viewing the "third world" as a way of opposing advances of the "second" or Marxist world. The recent rejection of Marxism by almost all second world countries makes the name "third world" irrelevant, and seems to settle a long, bitter debate between capitalist and Marxist systems.

But we would be deluding ourselves if we thought that our way of life had somehow been triumphantly vindicated. We are discovering rather that what capitalist and Marxist alike thought of as "development" may be impossible for the rest of the world. It may, in fact, prove disastrous for all of us, because it overlooks limits built into creation itself.

We can no longer assume that environment and development are separate issues. We have begun to hear a great deal about "sustainable development." The phrase is slippery, and people use it to justify many different things, but in principle it expresses a recognition that there are limitations to the planet, and that no people or country or region can "develop" economically or industrially in ways that surpass its carrying capacity. Christians ought to rejoice at this shift in attitude, for it contains an implicit recognition that we are creatures, not gods, and that we must learn to live as creatures, within limits imposed by the Creator. An important source of the idea of sustainable development was an in-depth United Nations study published in 1987 under the title *Our Common Future*. These words from the introduction of that book express the recognition that underlies the idea.

> Until recently, the planet was a large world in which human activities and their effects were neatly compartmentalized within nations, within sectors (energy, agriculture, trade), and within broad areas of concern (environmental, economic, social). These compartments have begun to dissolve. This applies in particular to the various global "crises" that have seized public concern, particularly over the past decade. These are not separate crises: an environmental crisis, a development crisis, an energy crisis. They are all one.... Ecology and economy are becoming ever more interwoven—locally, regionally, nationally, and globally—into a seamless net of causes and effects.[1]

Problems of Development. Here are some of the threads in that "seamless net" of environmental and developmental problems.

Human population growth is placing inexorable pressure on the fabric of creation. In 1980 there were 840 million more people in the world than in 1990; in the next ten years we will add about 960 million.

The gap between rich and poor is increasing. The rich are getting richer, and the poor are actually getting poorer. The "trickle down" myth—that the wealth of the very wealthy inevitably will lift the condition of the poor is a cruel lie in much of the world. Forty-three "developing nations" finished the decade of the 80s poorer than when they started it.

The cash flow from poor to wealthy nations is increasing. Till 1984, industrialized countries loaned more to poorer countries than they received in interest; since 1984 the poor have been paying more. In 1988 the poor were paying the rich fifty billion dollars per year on a debt of over a trillion dollars.

The debt load of poor nations is increasing. In order to meet the steadily growing needs for cash to make the interest payments (without which many major American and European banks would collapse), poorer countries are forced to place ever harsher demands on their land: through logging forests, growing cash crops like coffee and sugar, and inadvertently forcing the poor off the good land and onto marginal land. Farming on this marginal land inevitably increases erosion and destruction of wildlife habitats.

The poor are almost always the first to experience the consequences of degradations of creation. Meager food and dwindling firewood result from erosion, floods, and landslides from over-farming on steep slopes. The poor are increasingly forced off the farms and into the cities, where they encounter polluted water, dirty air, and dangerously crowded living conditions.

Television exports a wasteful, careless way of life. Even in the lowest levels of poverty, almost all of the world has access to television. What most of the world sees modeled on television is a North American or European way of life, in which people drive big cars and are careless of each other and creation.

What does this overwhelming collection of problems have to do with our own backyard?

What Can We Do?

Most important, we can become aware of the state of the planet and our contribution to that state. One of the best sources for sober, fact-filled analyses of the world situation is the "Worldwatch Papers," published by the Worldwatch Institute. These are summarized yearly (since 1984) in the *State of the World* reports, edited by Lester Brown (available from W.W. Norton Co., New York).

We should not get our news only from a North American viewpoint—and certainly not only from television, which is notoriously incapable of communicating complexities. Among easily available newspapers, the *Christian Science Monitor* remains one of the most consistently accurate on world news.

We can encourage the missions that our churches support to include the healing of creation in their proclamation of the gospel. We should not neglect the central announcement of the gospel, which is the reconciliation between people and their Creator; but neither can we forget that this central reconciliation should lead to reconciliation between rich and poor—and between humans and the rest of creation. (Unfortunately, there are many relief and development organizations that seek to bring reconciliation between people and creation without ever looking at the central reconciliation between persons and God.)

We need to see the seriousness of population growth and encourage restraint. We need to oppose both those who support population control at any price (including abortion) and those who say that it is not Christian to limit population. And though we should support population control in "developing" nations, we need to recognize our own responsibility in this area. Generally, as people's standards of living rise, the number of children per family tends to fall. Also, one North American child places as much burden on the fabric of creation as fifty from the poorest nations. More important perhaps, than limiting population growth, we should work particularly hard at developing and modeling ways of life that are not so wasteful of creation. Then our words about limiting population growth will have some weight.

ALL CREATURES

Right in the middle of the Bible a thoroughly troubled and tormented man asks his Creator why he has allowed such things to come upon him. Job's friends are horrified at his presumptuous complaints and tell him to let God alone. But Job keeps demanding an answer from his silent God. Finally God does reply. His answer is as astonishing to us as it was to Job. The Creator does not give reasons for his ways; instead he asks Job questions about creation. God gives Job a whirlwind tour of the cosmos. First he points out the vast world of star, stone, sea, and rain (see Job 38).

But the Creator reserves his greatest and most extensive delight for his living creatures (see Job 39) culminating in a two-chapter exultation on the beasts Behemoth and Leviathan. These were great untamable creatures which have been variously identified with the hippopotamus, the elephant, the whale, and the crocodile (see Job 40-41).

Two things are important for us in God's remarkable reply to Job. The first is that God cares about his creation a great deal. The second is that these creatures have value quite apart from any use we can make of them. In fact, God suggests that their value for Job is that he *can't* do anything with them: they are wild and free and remain completely outside the circle of human usefulness. They remind us of the Creator's exuberant power and creativity.

The same point is made elsewhere in the Bible: often in the Psalms; certainly in the story of the flood, where many of the passengers in the ark were animals of no practical use to humans; and in Jesus' words about the birds of the air, who are fed by their maker, and the sparrow, who does not fall outside of God's knowledge.

Yet we persist in acting as though creation were for us alone. It *is* "for us" in a special way: we are not just big-brained organisms in a cosmic dance with no center. But it is "for us" not only to use but to delight in. We have a particular responsibility to preserve all creatures, to mediate God's care to them. Looked at in this way, the casual way in which we acquiesce in the daily disappearance of whole species is a horrible perversion of our stewardship.

That is indeed what is happening to God's creation: in all sorts of ways we are diminishing its diversity, acting as though creatures had no value apart from their value to us. Although extinction is a part of creation, we have speeded up the process. It is most alarming in the rain forests. In these areas, comprising about two percent of the earth's surface, live over half of the species of plants, animals, and insects. At current rates, eighty percent of the rain forests will be gone by the turn of the century. We are letting their inhabitants be destroyed without even being known or named. More tragic than their disappearance is that many forest peoples who *have* known, named, and learned to make careful use of the great wealth of wild things often begin to to lose their knowledge when they are exposed to the Christian gospel and to Western civilization.

There are plenty of good human-centered reasons to be concerned about this vanishing of wild things. Much of the world's oxygen is produced by the rain forest, and burning it produces perhaps a quarter of the carbon dioxide emissions that are warming the planet. At least a quarter of our medicines come from rain forest plants, and these only from the small fraction of plants we've identified. But quite apart from human usefulness, the multitudinous wildness of the rain forest should be valuable to us simply because it is valuable to the Creator.

Here are some things we can do to develop our care for all creatures:

Care for a Pet. Even though cats and dogs have been a part of the human world for many thousand years, they still remind us that there are ways of being in the world that are quite different from our own—and yet which are intrinsically

Ghillean Prance, a Christian botanist (director of the Royal Kew Gardens) responding to the question, "What is it like to walk in a tropical rain forest?"

To begin with, it's wonderful that you *can* walk through it. The canopy cuts off nearly all sunlight, and in the shade only a few low plants can grow. The forest is very still. In the canopy you disturb screeching birds and hear buzzing hummingbirds and howler monkeys. You see tropical orchids—as many as forty species of flowers in one treetop—and brilliantly colored frogs, butterflies, and beetles. In contrast, the forest floor is much more sedate.

If you keep very still, you may hear the chirping of katydids or cicadas. Lie down on the moist soil and you can see ten species of ants, and sometimes exotically camouflaged insects. Often you will hear the sudden roar of rain, like a locomotive bearing down on you. At first you don't know the sound—you see, the forest canopy is so dense that it takes even the heaviest rain about ten minutes to filter through the vegetation. Then you'll feel the warm drops falling from the treetops 150 feet above.

To me the only thing comparable is the experience of walking into one of the great cathedrals such as we have in England. You are awed and humbled and stilled. You walk out purged by an almost sacred beauty. And when you leave, you are determined to defend that building, or that forest, at any cost.

—Philip Yancey "A Voice Crying in the Rain Forest," *Christianity Today*, July 22, 1991,(Vol. 35, No. 8), 28.

worthwhile. Developing a relationship with a cat, dog, bird, or goldfish is a good way for young and old to broaden their creaturely awareness and stewardship gifts.

Pets can be earthkeeping problems as well. Rare animals should never be taken from the wild and used as pets. Pets should be trained and controlled and given love and time so that they don't damage other plant or animal life. And pets need to be fed, sometimes taking resources from people. So own pets wisely, moderately.

Help Preserve Wild Areas. We need to support movements for the preservation of wilderness, both close to home and far away. Only little bits and pieces of creation are left undiminished by human activity. Till we have learned to treat them more carefully, the wisest course is probably not to use them at all—in some cases, not even for recreation.

Arguments that pit jobs against wilderness are usually not valid, since only a very small remnant is ever preserved as wilderness. The jobs are threatened anyway usually, by policies that pretend that the forest is inexhaustible. In the face of a deluge of human destructiveness, organizations like Friends of the Earth, the Audubon Society, the Wilderness Society, the Nature Conservancy, and Canadian Parks and Wilderness Society are good organizations for modern-day Noahs to support.

Shop with Creation Care. Don't buy or use products that threaten wild things. This ranges from obvious things, such as ivory or fur, to less obvious, such as objects made of imported tropical woods. (Some woods can be "farmed" in a way that leaves the forest intact; we probably should encourage their use.) These days, even fine-grained, old-growth fir or cedar is likely to diminish crucial habitat.

Refuse to buy tuna that is caught with a net that drowns dolphins. Look for a dolphin sign on your tuna can to indicate it is "dolphin safe."

Positively, we need to support products that provide creation-careful work and income for people in other countries. Even economically, the rain forest is most valuable as a healthy, diverse forest. Crops like Brazil nuts, some woods, and cacao (the source of chocolate) can be grown there without destroying the forest. Here, finally, is a good excuse to eat chocolate!

Companies like Patagonia are marketing nuts and candies which provide much-needed income to rain forest countries. Or you can buy a soft drink, Guarana (bottled in São Paulo, Brazil), made from rain forest fruits.

Support Creation-Minded Missions. We need to support missionaries who are in turn supportive of the indigenous cultures that care for creation. Ghillean Prance (the rain forest botanist quoted above) is particularly grieved by missionaries who have little sympathy for the vast and ancient knowledge of the forest that native peoples have: "These Indians live in a forest of enormous genetic diversity. We have studied scores of tribes in South America. The least efficient tribe utilizes fifty-six percent of all the trees for such products as medicine, clothing, food, and shelter. The most efficient uses every last species of tree. They've lived in harmony with the forest for centuries."[2]

Too often, when Christians bring the gospel to these people, they do not bring an appreciation of that knowledge of creation. So we need to encourage missionaries—and the church generally—to cherish and support all wisdom about how to use creation's gifts. For all creation should be brought into the new life in Christ.

Of many organizations that have been recently formed out of care for the rain forest, one of the best is **Rain Forest Alliance**, 270 Lafayette Street, Suite 512, New York, NY 10012 (212-941-1900).

ALL MONEY

A tithe of everything from the land, whether grain from the soil or fruit from the trees, belongs to the Lord; it is holy to the Lord.
—Leviticus 27:30

Many of the principles of caring for creation that we have outlined in this book don't cost anything, and even save us money. But many other ways of tending the "garden" of this earth require research, constant updating of information, and an organizational network. All of this takes money. Church bulletins, relief agencies, newsletters, and environmental groups all plead for our money, usually with good reason. So we often find ourselves in a quandary: which of many good causes should we support? The question takes us back to basic financial questions: how do we spend our money?

Some basic guidelines always help. The principles and suggestions here serve only as starting points for your own thinking and decisions about letting your money care for creation.

Follow the "Fifty-Fifty" Rule. If an organization is raising money to support a cause—whether it is supporting your church, preserving the rain forest, or providing food for refugees—insist that fifty percent or more of all that organization's income go directly to support that cause. If more than half of the income goes to expenditures of administration (including salaries, supplies, buildings) and information materials (advertising, printing, postage), then reconsider your support. Some organizations use up to ninety percent in such overhead; others get by on ten percent. Knowing this information should help you make better choices about how to spend your money.

A Tithe for Creation. One-tenth of our income—so we interpret scriptural teaching on tithing—is that portion of our gifts from God that we should give directly back to him. Of course, in one sense everything in creation, including our own lives belongs ultimately to God, which is why "stewardship" is such an important idea. In the Old Testament the tithe was "holy to the Lord"—given directly to the priest at the temple for maintaining the religious center for faith and life. Today our life and finances are more complicated, but we must not shortchange that center of our faith. We may find it tempting to reinterpret "tithe" to mean "gift to any benevolent cause," but our faith is not just one of many benevolent causes.

Schools, churches, and missions nurture and strengthen faith, both our own and that of others, so our tithe should go to these centers of our faith, not just any good cause. And we should demand of these churches and Christian organizations the highest level of stewardship.

We spoke previously about two kinds of Christian organizations: those whose main thrust is the preaching of personal salvation; and those which are working, in the name of Christ, for the healing of creation generally. Some groups do both, but not many. We should support both types. Here are three organizations that are solidly Christian and have a strong sense that the message of reconciliation is for both people and land.

—*Tierra Nueva:* 1 Birmingham Pl., Vernon Hills, IL 60061. This group is restoring land, agriculture, and people in the hill country of Honduras.

—*ECHO, Inc.* Educational Concerns for Hunger Organizations, 17430 Durrance Rd. North Fort Meyers, FL 33917, (813-543-3246). This organization researches and provides seeds for new food-producing tropical plants and supplies them mainly to missionaries and Peace Corps workers, who write their thank-yous with stories of the changes these seeds bring to the life of communities.

—The Mennonite Central Committee, 221 South 12th St., Box M, Akron, PA 17501 (717-859-1151). Founded in 1920, M.C.C. has a reputation the world over for demonstrating the love of Christ through a wide range of appropriate development projects, ranging from reforestation with native tree species in Kenya, to teaching Telagu slum-dwellers in Bombay how to use a sewing machine.

Beyond the Tithe: Charitable Giving. Our tithing in support of various Christian work should not exhaust our giving. Christians need to give both money and time to organizations that seek to bring healing and peace to creation. Sometimes non-Christians in these organizations have grasped a part of the gospel that Christians have neglected.

By our involvement we can counter a common misconception that Christians care only for "souls" and are gloomily glad about environmental degradation because it only proves that the end is near. It's important that people in these organizations know that it is "creation," not nature, we are caring for, and that the Creator's care for creation and for us is centrally seen in Jesus.

We also need to oppose a bizarre development: some environmental groups, out of a genuine concern for defenseless creatures, have been unequivocal supporters of abortion as a means of birth control. But in that support they favor the destruction of defenseless *human* creatures, encouraging real and present evil in the name of an abstract future good. We ought to criticize these policies. But our criticism will have more credibility if we support them in their concern for the life of nonhuman creatures.

In the Marketplace: Money Talks for Creation. For better or worse, money is one of the main means through which we use creation. What we support with our money (whether through magazine subscriptions, charge cards, or shopping lists) becomes a vote for or against a part of creation. And just as in politics, each vote means that the issue at hand is going to be taken more seriously. In a variety of ways we can start tipping dollars toward groups that are working for the care of creation. Government policymakers would then have ample proof that voters mean business (literally) on this issue, and businesses would realize that not just "eco-freaks" are concerned about products detrimental to wildlife. Here are some of these ways to spend money wisely for creation.

Subscribe to "environmental" magazines. These magazines not only give us information; their subscription list is a way of saying to advertisers that a lot of people care about the issues the magazines deal with. Such information sends ripples through the whole market system. And magazines are a good way of keeping in touch with threats to creation and ways of protecting it.

The best way to decide which ones to subscribe to is to go to the library and browse thoughtfully. Obviously, if you can get the information in the library, you don't need to subscribe yourself. But one of the main reasons for subscribing to some key magazines is that your home may itself become a kind of library for other people. Here are some we particularly recommend:

Audubon Magazine, National Audubon Society, Membership Data Center, P.O. Box 51000, Boulder, CO 80321-1000. About more than birds! *Audubon* is a grace to any coffee table, a pure joy visually for any page-thumber, and an excellent, balanced introduction to a wide variety of concerns. What we like is that the magazine (and the organization) maintains a healthy *joy* in creation while not minimizing *care;* also, part of the membership subscription goes to projects. The goal of the editor has been "to introduce a generation of readers to writing about natural history and conservation issues as *literature,* not merely information; to nature-photography and painting as *art,* not merely as pictures."[3] *Audubon* also publishes a newspaper for children called *Audubon Adventures.*

Garbage: The Practical Journal for the Environment, P.O. Box 51647, Boulder, CO 80321-1647. Full of good, up-to-date information on everything from leaky plumbing to backyard habitat restoration. Be forewarned, however; the ads will tempt you into eco-consumerism.

The National Geographic. The National Geographic Society, founded for "the increase and diffusion of geographic knowledge," has always been a good window on creation and human use of it. But the *Geographic* magazine has, in the past few years, become one of the best sources of information on the growing human impact on earth, sea, and sky—always, brilliantly illustrated with photos, maps, graphs, and drawings. (National Geographic Society, Box 2895, Washington, D.C. 20013 USA, or Box 2395, Postal Station A, Toronto, Ontario, Canada M5W 9Z9.)

ESA Advocate. The monthly newsletter of Evangelicals for Social Action, 10 Lancaster Ave., Wynnewood, PA 19096.

Evangelicals for Social Action does an excellent job of argu-
ing and lobbying for justice, including justice for the land.

And especially for children:

Owl: The Discovery Magazine for Children, Suite 304, 56th
Esplanade, Toronto, Ontario, Canada M5E 1A7. We feel
this to be the finest-quality introduction for children.

Ranger Rick (ages 6-12), *Your Big Backyard* (ages 3-5). Interesting and attractive nature magazines for children. Check
them out at your local newsstand.

Shop for the care of creation.

—Encourage local stores to stock creation-caring products.
Low-flow showerheads, fluoro-compact light bulbs, recycled paper, solar battery-chargers—all these creation-
friendly developments need to be for sale where anyone
can buy them easily.

—Support businesses that care for creation. Many hiking and
recreational equipment stores and co-ops fund projects
and organizations that are doing good work. Ask your
favorite stores of this type what they do to care for creation. After all, if it weren't for the beauty of the created
world and our joy in it, they wouldn't even be in business.

Patagonia is a good example (P.O. Box 150, Ventura,
CA 93002). As the company says in its cover-letter response
to requests for information about the Patagonia Environmental Tithing Program: "Many of you contacting us want
to know why we are donating to environmental causes. At
Patagonia we create clothing designed for rugged outdoor
use, therefore our commitment to preserving our nation's
wildlands for future generations is critical to us."

To support this policy, ten percent of the money it
receives for its products goes to support different environmental causes. Its lengthy yearly tithing list includes information about each group it has supported, and often
about the particular project its donation supported. And
its clothing fits its commitment: buttons from rain forest

tree seeds (for example) give work to inhabitants of existing rain forests. Both the work and the forests help to preserve indigenous culture.

—Let "plastic" money care for creation. Many organizations—such as the National Wildlife Federation and the National Audubon Society—have an arrangement with Visa or MasterCard for Affinity credit cards. Every time you use these cards a percentage of the service charge goes to the organization. Let your card care for creation by supporting the good work of one of these groups. Check the magazines at your local newsstand for up-to-date information.

No-Money Tithing. When we think of tithing we think of money. When the Bible speaks of tithe, it refers to it as "a tithe of everything from the land." The principle is repeated in the Leviticus law of letting the land lie uncultivated every seven years: effectively giving a seventh of the land back to the Creator. Since we're no longer an agricultural culture, we don't usually apply the words too literally. But caring for creation keeps bringing us back to the roots of our life, which are solidly sunk in the good earth. Even our discussion of money has constantly landed us back on earth, whether through seeds for missionaries, nature photography, or rain forest buttons. So this biblical principle of "a tithe from the land" raises intriguing possibilities.

Tithe from your garden. If you have a garden, take some of your produce to church, school, Bible study, or any meeting with friends and neighbors who have no garden. Who knows, they may get inspired to plant a plot of their own.

Tithe your own backyard. If you have a small garden area, use a tenth of it to grow something you know others would welcome. If you have a larger acreage, consider making some of it available to someone who would like to have a garden but has no place for it.

If you live in an apartment and think "this idea can't be for me," grow cuttings from your house plants or start fresh pots of basil and give these away to friends and neighbors. Mary Ruth's father, a professor, regularly gives African violets (grown in his windowless basement under Gro-lite bulbs) away to students, to brighten short winter days in the Chicago suburbs.

You might use one-tenth of your land as a wild area. Grow local plants and flowers in it.

ALL WORK

Teach Me, my God and King,
in all things thee to see,
and what I do in anything
to do it as for thee.

All may of thee partake;
nothing can be so mean,
which with this tincture, "For thy sake,"
will not grow bright and clean.

A servant with this clause
makes drudgery divine;
who sweeps a room as for thy laws
makes that an action fine.   —George Herbert

This book has been full of advice: some tentative, some dogmatic, but all of it making our life more complicated, giving us more work to do in an already busy life. With the whole of earthly creation entrusted to our care, we're easily mired by seeing the degradations of creation and by books like this on the hard work of caring for it. We get caught in the "mean" of daily drudgery and forget the goal: the "bright and clean" of a new creation.

The history of the Jewish people centers around this tension between the daily and the divine. Leviticus, with its intricate order of daily duties, strikes us as narrow and rigid. Yet these seemingly arbitrary rules were often crucial to health, family life, and justice. And most of the Old Testament is a record of lessons to learn, good and bad examples, and dire warnings—in fact a model for a what-to-do-and-how-to-do-it book like this one.

But in the middle of those sixty-six books, wedged in between the trials of Job on one hand and the pithy pointers of Proverbs on the other, is the long and wonderful collection of Psalms. This is a book of songs. We read songs of deliverance, songs in the night, new songs, songs with music, songs of praise. What kept these people singing was certainly not "the good life" or even basic justice, but rather the long and hard work of obedience. "Your decrees are the theme of my song wherever I lodge" (Ps 119:54). And that obedience is based on a deep sense that those decrees were established along with the heavens and the earth: indeed, they too are a part of creation:

> Your word, O Lord, is eternal;
> It stands firm in the heavens.
> Your faithfulness continues through all generations;
> you established the earth, and it endures.
> Your laws endure to this day,
> for all things serve you.   —Psalm 119:89-91

Our work then, as we care for creation, puts us in touch with the work of God. Sometimes the world looks so tainted that we cannot see the deep down freshness in the weed at the edge of the parking lot. To be able to work *and* sing we need to step back and see God's whole tapestry. Instead of looking at a tangled mass of threads, we need to re-member the perfect art of creation. We need to see the degradation of the parts but still keep our joy in the glory of the whole.

As we end all these suggestions for the work of caring for creation, we will—with yet more suggestions—attempt to shift our perception of that work. Hopefully in the end we'll be able to see the glory as well as the path, and sing songs of creation while we care for creation.

Remember the Meaning in the Menial. Most of the suggestions of these pages boil down to small actions: taking out the compost, turning off the lights, using the second side of a sheet of paper, turning the shower off while we soap up. While doing such duties it helps to remember the larger pattern. Each act of caring is not just daily drudgery, but a beginning of the new creation. Abraham Heschel, a great twentieth-century Jewish thinker, points out the centrality of the apparently trivial in God's action:

> The Bible insists that God is *concerned with everydayness, with the trivialities of life.* The great challenge does not lie in organizing solemn demonstrations, but in how we manage the commonplace. The prophet's field of concern is not the mysteries of heaven, the glories of eternity, but the blights of society, the affairs of the marketplace. He addresses himself to those who trample upon the needy, who increase the price of grain, use dishonest scales, and sell the refuse of corn (Amos 8:4-6). The predominant feature of the Biblical pattern of life is unassuming, unheroic, inconspicuous piety, the sanctification of trifles, attentiveness to details.[4]

Thus in these small acts of restoring a healthy creation we have as a model God himself: who created mosquitoes as well as hummingbirds; who uses centuries of drips to form the eerie and intricate beauty of caves; who uses snowflakes to carve mountains; and who as G.K. Chesterton reminds us, says to the sun every morning, "Do it again!"

"Think Globally, Act Locally." This popular bumper sticker is wise advice. Though we should be aware of global warming, species extinction, and the destruction of the rain forest, it's

Before you finish eating breakfast this morning, you've depended on more than half the world. This is the way our universe is structured.... We aren't going to have peace on earth until we recognize this basic fact of the interrelated structure of all reality.
—Martin Luther King Jr.

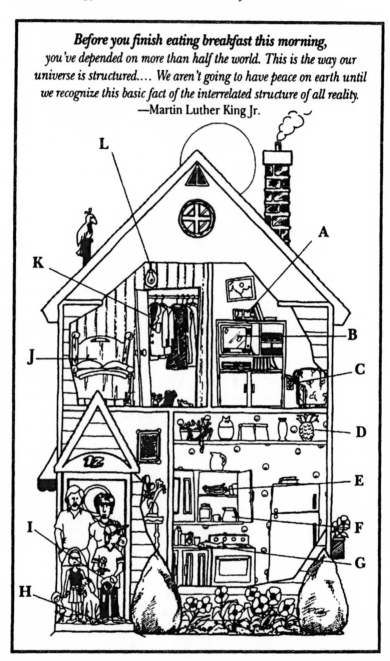

Who Are Our Suppliers?

A. Assembled in Taiwan. Workers earn less than 25 cents an hour.

B. Bastnaesite from Burundi. Life expectancy in Burundi is 42 years.

C. Electricity from coal mined in Clear Fork Valley, KY. About half of the residents live below U.S. poverty line; two-thirds have no flush toilets.

D. Pineapples from Philippines. One-half of children under four are afflicted by serious deficiency of proteins.

E. Meat, tuna, bananas from Somalia. Somalia has one of the greatest per capita food shortages in the world.

F. Coffee from Guatemala. Two-thirds of population has annual income of $42.

G. Cocoa and fish from Ecuador; 60 percent of children are malnourished. Sugar from Dominican Republic. 60 percent of children die before age five.

H. Rubber from Thailand. Per capita, Thais make $528 a year.

I. Baseball and glove from Haiti. Poorest nation in hemisphere; in a village of 6,000, average source of water is two taps. Infant mortality is one-of-five.

J. Teak furniture from Honduras. Honduras if the second poorest in the western hemisphere; 75 percent of Hondurans live in small, rural villages and earn an average $6 a month.

K. Clothes from Costa Rica. Workers earn less than 40 cents and hour.

L. Tungsten filament from Bolivia. A U.S. child will consume 30-50 times more good in his/her lifetime than one born in Bolivia highlands.

Other common items supplied by Third World nations: tea from Bangladesh; copper wiring from Chile; aluminum from Jamaica; tin from Malaysia; dog food from fishmeal from Peru; cork (for bulletin boards) from Algeria; natural gas from Mexico.

— *The Marketplace*, March/April 1991, 11

all too easy for these to become burdensome clichés. We need to start with the microcosm of our own homes and communities: that's where we'll make a difference. As Wendell Berry puts it, "Nearly every one of us, nearly every day of his life, is contributing *directly* to the ruin of this planet."[5]

We can't take on the cares of the whole creation, at least not all at once! Only God can do that—and does that, continually. It is not Atlas who bears the world on his shoulders, but Christ on the cross. That is the center of caring for creation.

Keep Singing. In all our work of saving, we can easily forget to notice the creation we are working to save. It is important to be able to delight in its perpetual novelty: to have a song every day for creation, to the Creator.

Morning has broken, like the first morning,
Blackbird has spoken, like the first bird.
Praise for the singing! praise for the morning!
Praise for them springing fresh from the Word.

Sweet the rain's new fall, sunlit from heaven,
Like the first dewfall on the first grass.
Praise for the sweetness of the wet garden,
Sprung in completeness where his feet pass.

Mine is the sunlight! mine is the morning
Born of the one light Eden saw play!
Praise with elation, praise every morning,
God's re–creation of the new day!

—Eleanor Farjeon

CONCLUSION: KEEP THE SABBATH

The meaning of the Sabbath is to celebrate time rather than space. Six days a week we live under the tyranny of things in space; on the Sabbath we try to become attuned to holiness in time. It is a day on which we are called upon to share in what is eternal in time, to turn from the results of creation to the mystery of creation, from the world of creation to the creation of the world.

—Abraham Heschel, *The Sabbath: Its Meaning for Modern Man*

○

Most Christians try to obey the Ten Commandments, but we often make an exception at the fourth one: "Remember the Sabbath day by keeping it holy" (Ex 20:8). Perhaps we are influenced by childhood memories of long, boring Sunday afternoons, or by prohibitions of things "not right" to do on Sunday. Perhaps we are offended by the old-fashioned nature of the commandment, its distinctly anti-modern tone. For in a world where economic efficiency is a central value and where economic survival is measured in a few percentage points of profit margin, it seems foolish to simply shut down entirely one day in seven. And, after all, isn't keeping the Sabbath a legalistic notion that Jesus himself repudiated?

It is good for us to recall that the Sabbath is a time in which all creation honors the Creator. This commandment is linked directly to creation: "For in six days the Lord made the heavens and the earth, the sea and all that is in them, but he rested on the seventh day." And central in the description of the Sabbath commandment is the idea that *all creatures* "within your gates" should experience the Sabbath rest.

Abraham Heschel, a twentieth-century Jewish scholar, points out that Judaism does not have a sacred place or places. It honors, rather, a sacred time: a time not related at all to the cycles of creation, but occurring every seven days, as if to remind us that the Creator is not contained in or limited by creation. The regular Sabbath observance reminds us of God's otherness; it also is a time when the Creator is felt to be particularly *present to* his creation. It is, as Heschel says, a "palace in time," when through the conscious observance by men and women, all things are recognized as a gift from God.

Christians should recall too that the author of the epistle to the Hebrews identifies Jesus as our Sabbath rest. And Jesus himself, when he took the scroll in the synagogue in Nazareth at the beginning of his public ministry, read from the ultimate Sabbath passage, Isaiah 61. He read Isaiah's description of the "Year of Jubilee"—the fiftieth year in which captives are freed and the broken are healed. Jesus said, "Today this Scripture is fulfilled in your hearing" (Lk 4:21).

All of this suggests that we need to remember the Jewish celebration of creation when we celebrate on Sundays the resurrection of Jesus, our Sabbath, the Lord of creation. We can certainly learn much from the traditional Jewish celebration of the Sabbath: the lighting of the Sabbath candles, the sharing in a Sabbath meal of the best of God's gifts, in a setting in which all of the creatures under our roof are at peace with each other and their Creator.

Perhaps we still need to keep the days distinct but closely related: the Sabbath, recalling the goodness of the old creation, and Sunday, which points all creatures eagerly forward to creation's renewal in Christ. Jurgen Moltmann's advice on a "Christian way of sanctifying the Sabbath" is good:

> It would be a useful practical step in this direction if the *eve* of Sunday were allowed to flow into a sabbath stillness. The Saturday evening devotions which are held in many congregations, and which many Christians like to attend, always unconsciously and involuntarily contain something of the rest and happiness of Israel's sabbath. After the week's work one comes to rest in God's presence, sensing on this evening something of the divine 'completion' of creation. Worship on Sunday morning can then be set wholly in the liberty of Christ's resurrection for the new creation. This worship should spread the messianic hope which renews life. Sunday will again become the authentic Christian feast of the resurrection if we succeed in celebrating a Christian sabbath the evening before.[6]

Here are some other suggestions for keeping the Sabbath of creation:

—Practice the discipline and delight of regularly saying no to ordinary work on Sunday. The Sabbath is a time of recognizing that our work is not ultimate: that God's work, completed in creation and redemption, is over all.

—Keep your driving to a minimum on the Sabbath. Though it became legalistic, the Hebrew conception of a "Sabbath day's journey" (only a short, refreshing walk) is a good one. Sunday is not a day to wear ourselves out with travel. Here's more good advice from Jurgen Moltmann. "The ecological day of rest should be a day without pollution of the environment—a day when we leave our cars at home, so that nature too can celebrate its Sabbath."[7]

—Resist attempts to carry on "business as usual" on the Sabbath. Stores should be closed and employees need a rest, not because they are Christians but because they are creatures. In our regular cessation from obsessive activity, we say for us and for all creatures, "The earth is the Lord's."

—Deliberately make the Sabbath a day of resting in and delighting in the gifts of creation. With food, fabric, flowers, this is the weekly time to remember creation's goodness.

Creation waits now for the gardener to speak:
And the eager weeds await their release
From the bondage of being weeds.
Eden and Zion lie far apart
But atom and ocean, beasts and plants
Wait for the one who will grant them peace.
Then the planet will spin in a Sabbath dance
(And the dancing place will be the heart).
Fruit will burgeon from scattered seeds
And garden and town be clean as a fleece
Early in the morning, on the first day of the week.

—Loren Wilkinson, from "Imago Mundi"

NOTES

ONE
Reduce

1. From Jon R. Luoma, "Even if Rich Shouldn't You Switch?" *Audubon*, (May 1991).
2. P. Poor, *Garbage* (March/April 1991), 36-37.

THREE
Recycle

1. Aldo Leopold, *Sand County Almanac* (New York: Ballantine Books, 1966), 111-112.

MEDITATION
Christmas and Creation

1. *St. Athanasius on the Incarnation*, trans. and ed. by A Religious of C.S.M.V. (New York: St. Vladimir's Orthodox Theological Seminary), 33.
2. G.K. Chesterton, "The House of Christmas," *The Collected Poems of G.K. Chesterton* (New York: Dodd, Mead and Co., 1980), 130.

FIVE
Fix It

1. Wendell Berry, "Why I Am Not Going to Buy a Computer," in *What Are People For* (San Francisco: North Point Press, 1990), 171-172.

SIX
Share It

1. C.S. Lewis, *The Screwtape Letters and Screwtape Proposes a Toast* (New York: The Macmillan Co., 1961), 109-110.

SEVEN
Planting

1. *Don't Worry, Plant a Tree*, by Ted Williams, *Audubon* (May 1991), 32.

EIGHT
Eating

1. Robert Farrar Capon, *The Third Peacock: A book about God and the problem of evil.* (New York: Image Books, 1972), 18.
2. These and other details about the chicken business come from chapter two ("Brave New Chicken") in *Diet for a New America* by John Robbins, (New Hampshire: Stillpoint Publishing, 1987) 48-72.
3. Robbins, 53.
4. Robbins, 81-82.

5. Cited in Robbins, 372.
6. John Robbins from *Diet for a New America*, cited in *Fifty Simple Things You Can Do to Save the Earth* (Berkeley, CA: The Earthworks Press, 1989), 90.
7. Wendell Berry, "Think Little," *A Continuous Harmony: Essays Cultural and Agricultural* (New York: Harcourt, Brace, Jovanovich, 1975), 77.
8. Cited in Robbins, 104.

NINE
Protecting

1. Thomas Howard, *Splendor in the Ordinary*, also published under the title *Hallowed Be this House* (Wheaton, IL: Tyndale House, 1976), 27–28.
2. Neil Postman, *The Disappearance of Childhood* (New York: Dell, 1984), 152.
3. Mary Catherine Bateson, "Caring for Children, Caring for the Earth," *Christianity and Crisis*, March 31, 1980, 70.
4. G.K. Chesterton, *Orthodoxy* (Image Books, 1959) 60.

TEN
Here: Learning to Be at Home

1. Adapted from Bill DuVall and George Sessions, *Deep Ecology: Living as If Nature Mattered* (Layton, UT: Peregrine Smith, 1985), 22-23. A yet earlier form of this quiz appeared in *CoEvolution*, no. 23 (Winter 1981).

TWELVE
Everywhere

1. *Our Common Future: The World Commission on Environment and Development* (Oxford: Oxford University Press, 1987), 4-5.
2. Ghillean Prance as per Philip Yancey, "A Voice Crying in the Rain Forest," *Christianity Today*, July 22 1991, (Vol. 35, No. 8).
3. *Audubon*, May 1991, 4.
4. Abraham Heschel, *I Asked for Wonder: A Spiritual Anthology*, edited by Samuel H. Dresner (New York: Crosssroad, 1990), 88-89.
5. Wendell Berry, "Think Little," *A Continuous Harmony* (New York: Harcourt, Brace, Jovanovich, 1975), 74.
6. Jurgen Moltmann, *God in Creation: A New Theology of Creation and the Spirit of God* (San Francisco: Harper, 1991), 296.
7. Moltmann, *God in Creation*, 296.

INDEX